FROM PLATO TO PIAGET

The Greatest Educational Theorists From Across the Centuries and Around the World

William Cooney, Ph.D., Philosophy
(Associate Professor, Briar Cliff College)

Charles Cross, Ph.D., Education
(Assistant Professor, Mount Union College)

Barry Trunk, Ph.D., Psychology
(Professor, Briar Cliff College, retired)

UNIVERSITY
PRESS OF
AMERICA

NATIONAL UNIVERSITY
LIBRARY SACRAMENTO

Lanham • New York • London

Copyright © 1993 by
University Press of America®, Inc.
4720 Boston Way
Lanham, Maryland 20706

3 Henrietta Street
London WC2E 8LU England

Library of Congress Cataloging-in-Publication Data

Cooney, William.
From Plato to Piaget : the greatest educational theorists from across
the centuries and around the world / William Cooney, Charles Cross,
Barry Trunk.
p.   cm.
Includes bibliographical references.
1. Education—Philosophy—History.   2. Education—Philosophy—
Terminology.   3. Educators—Philosophy—History.   I. Cross,
Charles.   II. Trunk, Barry.   III. Title.
LB14.7.C66   1993   370'.1—dc20   92–41787 CIP

ISBN 0–8191–9009–8 (cloth : alk. paper)
ISBN 0–8191–9010–1 (pbk. : alk. paper)

Dedication

We dedicate this work to our wives, all of whom exhibited a great amount of support and patience while this work was in progress:

Candace Cooney

Maria Cross

Kim Trunk

Acknowledgments

We wish to express our gratitude to the following for kindly granting permission to use copyrighted materials.

Washington Square Press/Simon & Schuster, Inc.

Teachers College Press/Columbia University

Houghton Mifflin Company

Georges Borchardt, Inc.

Ability Development

B.F. Skinner

CONTENTS

CHAPTER ONE

INTRODUCTION

The reader is about to embark on a journey through some of the greatest thoughts and ideas concerning education, from some of the greatest philosophers, psychologists and educators in history. And what could be a more fitting, more appropriate topic for these great minds to consider? Is not education itself the very cornerstone of everything else? How can a culture survive, much less grow and improve, if it has not learned how to educate its members? How will ideas be communicated and behaviors modeled, if we do not know how we should teach our young? Is anything more necessary, then, for the survival of human culture than education? The thinkers we are about to consult in our reading have a very profound understanding of the important role that education plays in our world. They come to us from different backgrounds, different cultures, and different times, often, to say the same thing: *that education, above all, is where we must start. Let us strive, therefore, to do it well!* All of our authors share the same goals and desires, but they come to us, primarily, from three disciplines: philosophy, psychology and education. It would be beneficial, therefore, for the reader to become at least briefly acquainted with the general outlines of these three disciplines and, in particular, how they interact with the great issues which concern education.

PHILOSOPHY

The discipline of philosophy began when ancient Greek thinkers like Thales (sixth century B.C.) attempted to answer new kinds of questions about the nature of the universe and about the human being's place in it. Heretofore, questions were approached on the level of the religious, mythical or poetic. One would look, for example, as an ancient Greek, to the writings of the poets Homer and Hesiod to discover clues about the world, the gods and the fate of humankind. Thales and others changed the very nature of the questions by demanding only those answers which were based in reasoned argumentation and on natural (rather than supernatural) foundations. The beginning of philosophy is also the beginning of science in the Western world, and in fact the first philosophers (the Presocratics) were involved in issues which would today be considered primarily scientific. Where did the universe come from? What is it made of? What are we made of? These were the kinds of questions they were asking. But the focus of philosophy was dramatically changed with the coming of Socrates (469-399 B.C.) who transferred the concern which had been a concentration on the external universe, to a concern about the interior universe, i.e., the soul or *psyche* of the human being. Socrates was not the first to consider this aspect of human nature, but he was the first to offer an organized look and consideration of such questions as: what is a human being? what does it mean to be a good or just human being? what is knowledge? what is justice? These kinds of questions are embodied in Socrates' great dictums "Know Thyself" and "The unexamined life is not worth living." And it was Plato who later continued this tradition handed down in the famous *Dialogues.*

Philosophy has had a very rich tradition during its more than twenty five hundred year history. A fuller treatment of this history would demand volumes. But the essential questions of philosophy can be fairly adequately summarized if we recognize the five major branches of the discipline. Each branch has many subdivisions, the following is merely an overview with an attempt to show the relationship to educational issues.

Logic is the study of correct thinking. This branch attempts to organize (Aristotle called logic the *organon*) correct rules of thinking and argumentation. Logic studies both deductive (deductive arguments claim that their conclusions follow from their premises with a degree of certainty) and inductive (inductive arguments claim only a degree of probability) forms of reasoning. Likewise, logic is divided into formal types of reasoning (symbolic logic) and informal types which are less symbolic and is more popularly dealt with under the rubric of "critical thinking." It is here that we can readily see the relationship of this branch of philosophy to education. How can one learn to think critically? How should we teach critical thinking? What is the relationship between critical thinking and other forms of thinking (for example, imaginative or artistic)? These are among the most important questions being asked and answered throughout the nation as it examines the state of education. No one denies the value of critical thinking. Neither do many deny that the status of current skills to do critical thinking is something to be openly concerned about. International conferences on critical thinking have emerged in the last several years as an attempt to address these concerns. There is now, in America, a National Council for Excellence in Critical Thinking (NCECT). Some recent research findings indicate that American students are not doing well in the area of reasoning and thinking. This is troublesome on many levels. On the very practical level, how can the United States expect to preserve its status as a "Superpower" if we continue to drop off in the areas of science and technology (both of which, of course, demand critical thinking skills)? Indeed, how can we expect to develop a sound economy for our children and maintain it, if we are falling behind in these areas? The research indicates that we are falling behind other nations in these areas, and the suspicion is centering around the various styles of education relevant to critical thinking.

But the real concerns, from the point of view of philosophy, are not on these practical, technological issues. Indeed, these sometimes lead to an isolationism and what is worse, an ethnocentrism (why should the U.S., for example be "the" superpower in the world?) which often divides people and leads to further ignorance rather than understanding. One of the reasons this text is written from a multicultural perspective, is a conviction that human growth and intelligence is best achieved when we see that we are all in this together. We encourage cooperative and collaborative models for learning and interacting. We can learn from each other. The whole concern about education derives from a "we" mentality rather than an "us versus them" view. The real concerns, therefore, from the philosophical viewpoint, are personal and human. How can we expect to engage with the questions of Socrates, if we cannot think critically about the very questions we ask and the answers we receive? Will we be able to determine the quality of those questions and answers? How will we be able to evaluate them? Indeed, if the distinctive feature of the human being lies in the ability to reason on a complex and higher level, it seems that critical thinking skills are by definition necessary in a human world. All of this, then, indicates the strong and very direct relationship that this branch of philosophy has with educational issues.

Epistemology is the study of knowledge. This branch also has an intimate relationship to education. What does it mean to know something for sure? How does one come to know something? What, in general, is learning theory? These are the direct questions being discussed today among the cognitive (learning) theorists in philosophy, psychology and education. Various models have been presented by leading theorists in this area, and some of the most notable cognitive theorists are among those that we consider in this text (James and Piaget, for example). The issues investigated by epistemology are fundamental to education. Education is about learning and epistemology is an investigation into how we best do that.

Aesthetics is the study of beauty. This branch of philosophy investigates issues concerned with the arts and music. What is art? What is beauty? These are the seemingly abstract questions that philosophers ask in this area. But they have a very practical application. We are constantly asking these questions everyday in the classroom (at least indirectly) when we consider works of art and music and encourage students to do art and music themselves. Art and music education is a very essential part of overall learning. Some, like Plato and Confucius, argue that they educate the soul just as the sciences, for example, educate the mind and the sports educate the body. The field of aesthetics has much to offer education in terms of establishing the dialogue about art and music in terms of trying to understand them both. Some see art and music education as somewhat of an inessential luxury. Others may see them useful if only because they indirectly improve our students ability in other areas (music education, for example, seems to facilitate the mathematical mind). But aesthetics argues that art and music education is an essential part of overall education in and by itself. Indeed, is not the appreciation of art and music a special, human feature?

Ethics is the study of behavior. This branch attempts to develop guidelines for appropriate, good or "right" behavior of individuals within a complex society. As a branch of philosophy, ethics goes beyond mere *description* and seeks to be *prescriptive.* The sociologist or anthropologist, for example, seeks to describe behavior. From this perspective, the goal is to learn about the variety of behavior patterns and customs from among the many cultures studied. But the mission of the sociologist/anthropologist usually includes only a descriptive study. No attempt is made, that is, to move from description to prescription. The philosopher, on the other hand, seeks to ask the prescriptive questions: After it is learned that culture A practices "shunning" for example, and that culture B does not, the philosopher seeks to discover if shunning is preferred behavior or not. Is shunning the kind of behavior we should prescribe? Under what circumstances? For which, if not all, cultures? These value-centered questions are, of course, not always easy to answer. But ethics is not a matter of looking for easy answers to difficult questions. Ethics attempts to provide various frameworks within which such difficult questions can be pursued.

Does the field of ethics have a relationship to education? It seems that there is an obvious connection. Many of the questions students are asked to think about either are directly ethical issues, or involve an indirect relation to ethical issues. When the student learns, for example, about the emergence of the United States of America as a nation initiated by the coming of white Europeans to an area already populated by native peoples with varied and already rich traditions, a tradition which was forcibly replaced by the dominant culture, certainly, ethical questions arise: was this fair? was it done with justice? is might always right?, etc. And many would argue that on a wider level, there is a need for education is character, as well as education in knowledge. Many of the thinkers we will be studying would agree with this proposition. Indeed, the survival of a culture very much depends on the quality of its character, and many suggest, that our educational system is not only wanting in critical thinking skills, it is also in need of a new direction in terms of moral or ethics education. Some of this is already being done in the various "values-clarification" techniques utilized within education. But most philosophers would argue that much more is needed than this, if we are to adequately respond to this growing need. Some nations, China and Japan, for example, regularly include moral/ethics education within the classroom setting. Universities and college across America, too, are turning to an ethics-across-the-curriculum program in growing numbers.

Metaphysics is the study of being or reality. This branch considers questions such as: what is the human mind like? are individuals free in their behavior, or determined by outside forces beyond their control (environment, genetics, etc.)? Metaphysics also concerns itself with religious issues: Is their a God? Is the universe the result of divine intervention? Is their a soul which survives the death of the body? etc. Some of these issues are never directly dealt with, of course, with the school system (at least not within the public school system which protects church and state separation), but some of them are relevant issues to consider within education. The nature of the mind, for example, and the questions about freedom and determinism come to mind here. Concerning the former, it seems obvious that educators should be interested in what metaphysics has to say in this area. Concerning the latter, some provocative issues arise. Suppose that we conclude that our personality, for instance, is largely the product of environmental forces outside of our individual control (this is the position, for example, of Skinner). Would this not dictate a wider concern with the kinds of environments we present to our children within the context of education? More than a few of the theorists we will study in this text suggest that we have a long way to go in this regard. Should we expect children from challenging environments (the ghettos, for example, or abusive environments at home) to be as motivated and able to participate in the classroom as those children which are privileged to have a loving, warm, helpful environment? Since it directly impacts how education will work, it seems that educators need to be concerned with such issues.

The various branches of philosophy, therefore, present many issues directly and indirectly related to education. It is not surprising, therefore, that many of the first educational theorists (like Plato) were philosophers, and that many of the great theorists of the present century (like Dewey) are philosophers.

PSYCHOLOGY

The science of psychology began as a formal discipline in the year 1879 when Wilhelm Wundt established the first psychological laboratory at the University of Leipzig, Germany. This new science was actually a merger between the fascinating questions posed by the philosophers and the scientific methodology of the physiologists of the day.

Psychology differed from philosophy not so much in the kinds of questions it raised, but rather in the methods it used to discover the answers.   In particular, psychology wanted to be a science, and its method became the scientific method based on experimentation and the testing of hypotheses.   In using this method, psychologists became successful in the description and prediction of behavior, and in the manipulation of the environment which produces, in a cause and effect way, that behavior.

Like philosophy, the science of psychology can be divided into five major perspectives.   Let us briefly consider each and make some preliminary suggestions concerning how each might contribute to the field of education.

Physiological psychology attempts to explain human and animal behavior through an understanding of the biological basis for it.   This perspective is especially interested in the workings of the brain, as well as the nervous and endocrine systems.   Physiological psychologists believe that complex human behaviors will eventually be best described at the level of the neuron (inside of the brain).   They are also interested in the effects of drugs, especially at the neural level, on the treatment of various psychological disorders.

As applied to education, this view calls our attention to the science of the brain itself.   For example, the two sides of the brain (hemispheres) do not perform identical functions.   In most people the left side of the brain excels at language, mathematics, and general reasoning ability, while the right side seems more equipped to deal with artistic, musical, and spatial data.   Educational techniques should, therefore, take account of this information in order to help create more well-rounded and integrated individuals.

Psychoanalytic psychology was fathered by Sigmund Freud (1856-1939) who suggested that there are forces that lie below the level of our conscious awareness (preconscious and unconscious forces). These forces have, according to this view, tremendous influences on our outward behaviors. In order, therefore, to understand the individual and his or her actions, we must penetrate into the deeper layers of the unconscious mind. Freud also postulated three structures within the personality: the ID, which creates unconscious and incessant demands to satisfy the needs of the body; the EGO, which strives to meet the demands of the ID and at the same time deal with the real world outside the ID; and, finally, the SUPEREGO, which serves as a powerful form of moral conscience to the EGO. In the normal individual, these three function in harmony. On the other hand, an imbalance of these will cause mental illness (an out of control ID characterizes an individual unable to resist temptation; a too dominant SUPEREGO can make one unable to really enjoy life without moral persecution). Freud also proposed the theory of "defense mechanisms" wherein an individual who may be facing anxiety often resorts to a rationalization (thus making excuses for oneself) or a projection (thus attributing one's own faults to someone or something else). In both cases, there is a real failure to face the problem directly.

While Freud did not directly study educational issues, many of his ideas can be applied. Freud's ideas about the unconscious forces on our outward behaviors, for example, needs to be considered. Education, after all, seeks to bring about behaviors in the classroom which will stimulate growth and development. Likewise, his theory of defense mechanisms should be taken into account by educators. All teachers have become familiar with the child who rationalizes that one need not care about geometry, or the child who projects his poor performance on to the supposed inabilities of the teacher. Freud's theories have also clearly established the importance of the first five years of childhood, and of the quality of the home environment.

Yet a third major force is **Behavioral** psychology which stresses the scientific and objective features of investigation. It rejects, therefore, all those aspects of the world and of our behaviors which are not objectively observable. This would include much of psychoanalytic psychology: the ID, EGO and SUPEREGO are not subject to observation, measurement and manipulation. Advocates like John Watson (1878-1958) and B.F. Skinner (1904-1991) conducted numerous experiments, both with animals and with people, in order to directly understand the relationship between the rewarding and punishing aspects of the environment and the behavior of the organism.

Skinner's ideas have directly impacted upon educational theory. His "Operant Conditioning" theory, in particular, has formed the basis for some theories of learning. According to this theory, the individual acts (operates) on the environment and causes a consequence to occur. Simply put, those behaviors which result in rewarding consequences are strengthened, and those which result in punishing effects are weakened and gradually extinguished over time.

While the theory is more complex than we are tracing here, one can already gain an idea of its utility in the classroom. The teacher and the school environment in general, can be either rewarding or punishing to the student. Praise may make a student feel like repeating the desired behaviors, while ridicule and failures may cause the child to retreat and become withdrawn (perhaps even producing antisocial behavior).

Cognitive psychology emphasizes an understanding of the decision-making processes and thinking strategies tied to behavior. People do not just respond unthinkingly to the environment. There is a complex network of information processing that occurs beforehand. The cognitive approach has increased in popularity and acceptance in recent years within the United States and elsewhere around the world. Psychologists like Albert Bandura (b. 1925) and Jean Piaget (1896-1980) have had a major impact in furthering this approach which is seen by many as a shift away from behaviorism.

Piaget was a brilliant scientist with a keen interest in childhood learning and thinking. For several decades Piaget and his colleagues carried out hundreds of experiments and observations on children. The wealth of data produced led Piaget to believe that cognitive growth can best be described as an active process occurring during four major stages. Within each of these stages the child takes in information through the senses and compares it to information they already have stored (assimilation). The child may need to modify or alter stored information in order to fully understand the world (accommodation). The two-step process of assimilation and accommodation leads to a state of cognitive equilibrium, which is a constant and ongoing process. Piaget's theories have, obviously, a very direct impact on learning theory, and have been adopted by many teachers with positive results.

Finally, **Humanistic** psychology evolved out of a dissatisfaction with both the Freudian and behavioral views. These were felt to be pessimistic and dehumanizing in not rightly recognizing the <u>uniqueness</u> of the human being. The humanists were quick to point out that the human being is special and ought to be studied with that assumption in mind. They were more interested in helping individuals to realize and actualize their own, unique potentials. Of the many contributors to this view, Abraham Maslow (1908-1970) and Carl Rogers (1902-1987) have had the most profound effects.

Maslow is best remembered for his "Hierarchy of Needs" theory. According to this view, unless the individual first satisfied the lower needs (physical: food, shelter, safety, etc.) the higher needs could not be fulfilled (psychological: love, self-esteem and self-actualization). Self-actualization is the goal that every individual should seek in striving to achieve their potentials. Since education seeks to bring about the self-

actualization of students, Maslow's theories have had a very
popular effect.

Rogers was sympathetic to Maslow's views but addressed
the issue in a different way. For Rogers, the notion of the
complete acceptance of an individual for what they are
(Unconditional Positive Regard) would allow that person the
freedom to become what they must become. This would enable
them to truly become themselves rather than what others want
them to be (suiting others but never themselves). Rogers
spoke of the internal need to merge our "Ideal Self" (what we
strive to be) with our "Actual Self", which is what we currently
are. As we become what we want to be, our actual and ideal
selves come closer and closer. The result is a fully functioning
and mentally healthy individual. Certainly teachers must keep
in mind the uniqueness and individuality of their students, and
resist the temptation to mold them into simply a carbon copy
of everyone else. Rogers' ideas have impacted education in the
promotion of an atmosphere of trust, warmth and
unconditional positive regard.

EDUCATION

Since the publication of *A Nation at Risk* in 1983,
American schools have moved through a decade of reform.
Issues such as quality, equity, accountability, and performance
expectations for both students and teachers, have been the
driving forces of the effort to improve education. At the heart
of this reform movement has been the struggle by educators,
administrators, politicians, business leaders and citizens in
general, to define a body of thoughts and ideas about
education; i.e., an educational philosophy. Consideration has
been given to questions such as: what is knowledge? what is
an educated individual? what is good schooling? how should
teaching be done? what are the ultimate purposes or goals of
education?

These issues are not unique to the recent school reform movement, nor is educational reform a concept which has only come to light in recent years. As long as humans have attempted to communicate ideas, thoughts and information to younger generations, there has been an attempt to grapple with the issues of education. In coming to terms with these issues, four educational schools of thought have emerged to shape the face of American school systems as well as educational systems around the world. We will now briefly examine these four schools of educational philosophy, hoping to display the different approaches which educators have taken in order to bring about the creation or development of the educated individual.

Perennialism views nature, knowledge, and the values of society as perennial, constant, and undergoing little or no change. The intellect of the individual is cultivated, according to this view, and strengthened through the exposure to truth as it is found in nature and in the recurrent themes of human existence. Based on principles derived from the medieval philosopher Thomas Aquinas (d.1274), perennialists believe that knowledge of the values and cultures of earlier societies have lasting benefit to today's world.

The goal of education, then, is not to achieve immediate gratification and satisfaction of only temporary needs, but the development of the disciplined mind. Perennialists believe that this is best achieved through exposing the student to traditional subjects, like the three R's in elementary school, and history, language, mathematics, literature, humanities, science and art at the secondary level. These traditional fields of study, it is argued, provide the mental exercise which will allow the individual to develop reasoning skills and and to become a rational individual. The teacher is seen as an authority figure, dispensing truth and knowledge to the students.

Emphasis on the enduring classics of Western culture has served as the foundation of the perennialist philosophy. The Paideia Proposal, submitted by the contemporary philosopher Mortimer Adler, is a current sample of this perennialist view. Adler reiterates that the "Great Book" approach, which he developed along with Robert M. Hutchins, would benefit all students by equalizing any socio-economic differences and uplifting every individual. This approach has, however, been criticized for its rigidity and inflexibility in determining what is worthy to be called "classical" and therefore suitable for instruction. In more recent years, this view has been charged with promoting only the "Eurocentric" view of intellectual thought, ignoring the contributions from non-European cultures.

Essentialism is the educational philosophy developed by people like William C. Bagley, and which seems to dominate in the American school system. The essentialists believe that there is a core of essential skills and information which every individual must possess in order to be an intelligent, successful, and learned member of society. They see this as a very practical, pragmatic and common sense approach to education.

The responsibility of the school, they argue, is to produce students that are prepared to be informed, active citizens, and reliable, trustworthy and qualified workers. Teachers are seen as authority figures and disciplinarians uniquely qualified to implement a curriculum that stresses the basic fundamental skills and understandings. Emphasis is placed on traditional methodologies and subject matter, with particular attention on mathematics and natural science. Through discipline, hard work, and respect for authority, students would develop factual mastery of the world and an ability to organize content and information. This would result in the self-discipline and an understanding of how to live life successfully. The acquisition of content or subject matter is considered much more important than the consideration of the learner's personal needs, interests, or motivations. There is also an emphasis on formalized testing and evaluation.

P r o g r e s s i v i s m, sometimes referred to as "experimentalism", views ⌐human nature, knowledge and truth as constantly changing. Unlike the perennialists, progressives like John Dewey and William James believed that knowledge must constantly be rediscovered and redefined. The value of knowledge, they argue,⌐resides in the ability to solve human problems and should be employed to redesign and improve upon the world.⌐

Progressivists reject the authoritarian approach of telling learners what and how to think, and replace this with the goal of teaching students how to think for themselves. The interest, furthermore, is on process rather than product. The teacher is seen as a facilitator, guiding learners through a student-centered, experience-rich curriculum designed to emphasize experimentation, human experience, socialization, and the development of problem-solving abilities. The school as a social institution, should serve as a working model of democratic society. Emphasis on learning strict subject matter is rejected as the traditional disciplines are employed as a point of departure for experience-based instruction which provides problem-solving methodologies. Textbooks and other learning materials serve as tools for learning, not absolute, indisputable sources of truth.

Two contemporary views closely related to this philosophy are reconstructionism and futurism. Like progressivism, these views concern themselves with preparing individuals to deal with the real world. Reconstructionists stress the need for social involvement in an interdependent, global community, desperate for social change. This movement sees itself as much more affective than progressivism, in producing learners that are not only prepared to be members of society but also reformers and activists that will help to change and transform our social structures. The futurists move beyond reconstructionism to stress preparation for and participation in a society with many unknowns. In a rapidly changing world, they argue, individuals must be prepared to meet new and unexpected challenges with the skills and abilities that can be adapted to changing circumstances. Students will have to learn to be independent thinkers, capable of making creative, ethical decisions to as yet unforseen problems.

Finally, **Existentialism** is a philosophy of education which stresses the achievements of individual self-fulfillment. Existentialists like Jean-Paul Sartre (1905-1980) believed that every person is first and foremost an <u>individual</u> (rather than simply a member of a group or "crowd"). The purpose or goal of life, then, is the quest for individual or personal meaning as one attempts to create one's life. According to this view, people cannot achieve personal meaning by being confined to preexisting and "orthodox" beliefs, philosophies, or dogma. The existentialists strongly emphasize the freedom of individuals to make their own choices and to determine their own direction in life.

This philosophy seems to run counter to the persistent effort in American school systems to emphasize group processes and group norms. The existentialists reject the traditional approach which they feel minimizes individual differences and perpetuates existing culture, reiterating perennially held beliefs and the status quo. The existentialist model stresses individual and personal fulfillment and self-actualization. Students are encouraged to explore, take chances, make choices, and arrive at their own answers. Teachers implement an affective approach which addresses student needs, interests, and motivations. Authoritarian pressure is removed and students are encouraged to research, formulate, express, and defend their own points of view. According to the existentialist, education exists not to indoctrinate, but to enable each person to follow their own nature.

This concludes our look at the major disciplines of philosophy, psychology, and education.   The thinkers we are about to encounter will represent one or other of these disciplines in far greater detail.   In point of fact, these thinkers will often represent an intersection between all three of these areas.   Theories of education inevitably offer us a philosophy which serves as an underpining, and a psychology which provides a theory about development and growth of the individual.   It is important for educators to at least think about the major philosophical and psychological ideas relevant to educational theory in general.   We believe that teachers who have a well developed philosophy and psychology of education, will have better focus and purpose in the classroom, as well as the intellectual tools to carry those goals out.   It is our hope that the selections which follow will serve the purpose of helping teachers to develop their own educational theories, and to help us all to better understand what education is and why it is so critically important.

CHAPTER TWO

PLATO

The important Greek philosopher Plato (427-347 B.C.) was in many ways the first great educator. He was not, of course, the first teacher in the West. The sophists were wandering teachers in Greece a full century before him. Plato's mentor, Socrates, also certainly was a teacher of importance not only to Plato, but to western civilization as a whole. But Plato can be given credit for being the first to rigorously formalize education in the West. He started the first real institution of learning which he called the Academy (this is where we get our word "academics"). Today, this institution is regarded as the first university. It was a place of learning on a scale heretofore unchallenged. Many subjects were taught, from mathematics and other sciences, to the arts of debate and the various areas of philosophy. The teachers at the Academy were highly regarded authorities in their respective fields, and came from other parts of Greece and beyond to teach. The students were also many and talented, the most famous of which was Aristotle. The Academy lasted as a great institution of learning for more than 900 years being closed finally by the Emperor Justinian in A.D. 529. No institution before or since has lasted that long.

Plato was also really the first thinker in the Western world, to offer a systematic, comprehensive theory of ideas about education (i.e., a *philosophy of education*). In his *Republic* Plato sets the goal of designing the most just kind of society. What would it be like? What laws would be enforced? What kind of lives would its citizens lead? How would the divisions of power be delivered out? All these questions and more are discussed with remarkable clarity and rigorous detail. Among these very important questions, Plato considers the fundamental issues of education. How will citizens of the just society be educated? Plato recognized the *fundamental* nature of this question. He was aware, that is, that nearly everything else depends on how we answer this question.

Plato begins with the conviction that the kind of society we construct for ourselves ought to be consistent with the kind of creatures human beings are. The State, he said, should in fact be "Man writ large." In other words, society should mirror and reflect human nature. He believed that human beings have a social nature and therefore that society is natural and not an artificial human convention. Human beings are the kinds of creatures that *need* society. The social structures offered in a State certainly help to shape and influence human nature. And the social structure of education is incredibly important because, he says, "the beginning is the most important part of any work, especially in the case of the young and tender thing; for that is the time at which the character is being formed and the desired impression is more readily taken."

Plato was vividly aware, then, of making a good start. Education is where we make our start. It is vitally important, therefore, that we take great care in designing it. Furthermore, Plato was also conscious of the reciprocal feature and relationship between the individual and society, and the role education can play. Society gets "paid back" by educating its citizens rightly and truly because education is a means, he thought, towards producing a "noble" character. As he put it, education makes "the soul of him who is rightly educated graceful . . . true education of the inner being will [make the student] noble and good." Plato goes on to conclude that "true education, whatever that may be, will have the greatest tendency to civilize and humanize them in their relations to one another . . . ." So education furthers the social character of our human natures and contributes in important ways to our nurturing. Society does have the duty, Plato was convinced, to nurture its citizens. And nurture and education, he felt, go hand in hand. "For good nurture and education," he wrote, "implant good constitutions, and these constitutions taking root in a good education improve more and more, and this improvement affects the breed in man as in other animals."

So then, according to Plato, education will be a major function of the State, and the State, in turn, will be the major *benefactor* of education. This is an idea we still hear debated in our own day. Should the State fully support education? What about all those tax dollars? What is really in it for us? For Plato, the State has everything to lose or gain depending on how well it supports education. It is very much in society's interest to support it well.

Plato offers many ideas about how education would be shaped in a just society. Some of his ideas are attractive to many and seen as innovative, others are quite controversial indeed. As an example of the former, consider that Plato rejects a long-standing patriarchal society when he argues that in a just society, women will be educated equally with men. Women, he says, "must have the same nurture and education." Certainly there are differences between men and women that Plato was well aware of. But he argues that these differences are not relevant to the question of how society should educate women. For example, he says, "if the difference consists only in women bearing and begetting children, this does not amount to a proof that a woman differs from a man in respect of the sort of education she should receive . . . ." And given that men and women are to be educated equally, should they both be eligible to equal stations in mature life? Should women, for example, be allowed to hold positions of authority in the just State? Again Plato answers affirmatively: "offices are to be held by women as well as by men." So many would find Plato's ideas here very progressive and remarkable especially for a thinker writing some 2,300 years in the past.

But there is also much controversy raised in Plato's *Republic* as well. For example, those disapproving of communal lifestyles will not like many of his plans for the most just State. Property will be shared in common, just as education should be. And the family unit will be replaced with a communal family structure where every adult sees every child as their responsibility. Likewise, those skeptical about censorship within society will disagree with Plato's intent to highly censor the system of education. The young, he felt, were especially impressionable in their characters. The just State, therefore, will censor the ideas taught in the arts and literature, for example.

Plato was very supportive, however, of the arts, literature, and the sciences, as well as of music and physical education. There should be "gymnastic for the body" he says, "and music for the soul." Together the two can contribute to a desired harmony between the body and soul of the person. Addressing both sides of our human nature is, after all, the true goal of education.

The reading which follows is taken from the seventh book of Plato's *Republic*. This section is known as "the cave allegory", and is among the most widely read parables in world literature. Here Plato speaks in simile and metaphor about seeking and achieving true understanding or enlightenment. The cave allegory is in many ways a summary of Plato's entire philosophy and is, therefore, not limited to issues concerning education. The story is also tied to the life and struggles of Socrates' who was executed by the State of Athens in 399 B.C. because of his ideas and desires to communicate them to others. But Plato himself, at the end of the story, specifically draws conclusions concerning the philosophy of education. Read in this light, the allegory speaks to what true education is, and of the responsibilities of each educated person to help to educate others, even at a great price to their own selfish goals and desires. The story is told as a dialogue led by Socrates.

PLATO'S CAVE: ON BREAKING THE CHAINS OF IGNORANCE*

And now, I said, let me show in a figure how far our nature is enlightened or unenlightened:--Behold! human beings living in an underground den, which has a mouth open towards the light and reaching all along the den; here they have been from their childhood, and have their legs and necks chained so that they cannot move, and can only see before them, being prevented from turning round their heads.   Above and behind them a fire is blazing at a distance, and between the fire and the prisoners there is a raised way; and you will see, if you look, a low wall built along the way, like the screen which marionette players have in front of them, over which they show the puppets.

I see

And do you see, I said, men passing along the wall carrying all sorts of vessels, and statues and figures of animals made of wood and stone and various materials, which appear over the wall?   Some of them are talking, others silent.

You have shown me a strange image, and they are strange prisoners.

Like ourselves, I replied; and they see only their own shadows, or the shadows of one another, which the fire throws on the opposite wall of the cave?

---

* **Source**: Plato, **The Republic**--Book VII, in *The Dialogues of Plato*, ed. Justin D. Kaplan (New York: Washington Square Press, 1950).   Reprinted by permission.

True, he said; how could they see anything but the shadows if they were never allowed to move their heads?

And of the objects which are being carried in like manner they would only see the shadows?

Yes, he said.

And if they were able to converse with one another, would they not suppose that they were naming what was actually before them?

Very true.

And suppose further that the prison had an echo which came from the other side, would they not be sure to fancy when one of the passers-by spoke that the voice which they heard came from the passing shadow?

No question, he replied.

To them, I said, the truth would be literally nothing but the shadows and the images.

That is certain.

And now look again, and see what will naturally follow if the prisoners are released and disabused of their error. At first, when any of them is liberated and compelled suddenly to stand up and turn his neck round and walk and look towards the light, he will suffer sharp pains; the glare will distress him, and he will be unable to see the realities of which in his former state he had seen the shadows; and then conceive some one saying to him, that what he saw before was an illusion, but that now, when he is approaching nearer to being and his eye is turned towards more real existence, he has a clearer vision,-- what will be his reply? And you may further imagine that his instructor is pointing to the objects as they pass and requiring him to name them,--will he not be perplexed? Will he not fancy that the shadows which he formerly saw are truer than the objects which are now shown to him?

Far truer.

And if he is compelled to look straight at the light, will he not have pain in his eyes which will make him turn away to seek refuge in the objects of vision which he can see, and which he will conceive to be in reality clearer than the things which are now being shown to him?

True, he said.

And suppose once more, that he is reluctantly dragged up a steep and rugged ascent, and held fast until he is forced into the presence of the sun himself, is he not likely to be pained and irritated? When he approaches the light his eyes will be dazzled, and he will not be able to see anything at all of what are now called realities.

Not all in a moment, he said.

He will require to grow accustomed to the sight of the upper world. And first he will see the shadows best, next the reflections of men and other objects in the water, and then the objects themselves; then he will gaze upon the light of the moon and the stars and the spangled heaven; and he will see the sky and the stars by night better than the sun or the light of the sun by day?

Certainly.

Last of all he will be able to see the sun, and not mere reflections of him in the water, but he will see him in his own proper place, and not in another; and he will contemplate him as he is.

Certainly.

He will then proceed to argue that this is he who gives the season and the years, and is the guardian of all that is in the visible world, and in a certain way the cause of all things which he and his fellows have been accustomed to behold?

Clearly, he said, he would first see the sun and then reason about him.

And when he remembered his old habitation, and the wisdom of the den and his fellow-prisoners, do you not suppose that he would felicitate himself on the change, and pity them?

Certainly, he would.

And if they were in the habit of conferring honours among themselves on those who were quickest to observe the passing shadows and to remark which of them went before, and which followed after, and which were together; and who were therefore best able to draw conclusions as to the future, do you think that he would care for such honours and glories, or envy the possessors of them? Would he not say with Homer, *'Better to be the poor servant of a poor master and to endure anything, rather than think as they do and live after their manner.'*

Yes, he said, I think that he would rather suffer anything than entertain these false notions and live in this miserable manner.

Imagine once more, I said, such an one coming suddenly out of the sun to be replaced in his old situation; would he not be certain to have his eyes full of darkness?

To be sure, he said.

And if there were a contest, and he had to compete in measuring the shadows with the prisoners who had never moved out of the den, while his sight was still weak, and before his eyes had become steady (and the time which would be needed to acquire this new habit of sight might be considerable) would he not be ridiculous? Men would say of him that up he went and down came without his eyes; and that it was better not even to think of ascending; and if any one tried to loose another and lead him up to the light, let them only catch the offender, and they would put him to death.

No question, he said.

This entire allegory, I said, you may now append, dear Glaucon, to the previous argument; the prison-house is the world of sight, the light of the fire is the sun, and you will not misapprehend me if you interpret the journey upwards to be the ascent of the soul into the intellectual world according to my poor belief, which, at your desire, I have expressed-- whether rightly or wrongly God only knows. But whether true or false, my opinion is that in the world of knowledge the idea of good appears last of all, and is seen only with effort; and, when seen, is also inferred to be the universal author of all things beautiful and right, parent of light and the lord of light in this visible world, and the immediate source of reason and truth in the intellectual; and that this is the power upon which he would act rationally either in public or private life must have his eye fixed.

I agree, he said, as far as I am able to understand you.

Moreover, I said, you must not wonder that those who attain to this beatific vision are unwilling to descend to human affairs; for their souls are ever hastening into the upper world where they desire to dwell; which desire of theirs is very natural, if our allegory may be trusted.

Yes, very natural.

And is there anything surprising in one who passes from divine contemplations to the evil state of man, misbehaving himself in a ridiculous manner; if, while his eyes are blinking and before he has become accustomed to the surrounding darkness, he is compelled to fight in courts of law, or in other places, about the images or the shadows of images of justice, and is endeavouring to meet the conceptions of those who have never yet seen absolute justice?

Anything but surprising, he replied.

Any one who has common sense will remember that the bewilderments of the eyes are of two kinds, and arise from two causes, either from coming out of the light or from going into the light, which is true of the mind's eye, quite as much as of the bodily eye; and he who remembers this when he sees any one whose vision is perplexed and weak, will not be too ready to laugh; he will first ask whether that soul of man has come out of the brighter life, and is unable to see because unaccustomed to the dark, or having turned from darkness to the day is dazzled by excess of light. And he will count the one happy in this condition and state of being, and he will pity the other; or, if he have a mind to laugh at the soul which comes from below into the light, there will be more reason in this than in the laugh which greets him who returns from above out of the light into the den.

That, he said, is a very just distinction.

But then, if I am right, certain professors of education must be wrong when they say that they can put knowledge into a soul which was not there before, like sight into blind eyes.

They undoubtedly say this, he replied.

Whereas our argument shows that the power and capacity of learning exists in the soul already; and that just as the eye was unable to turn from darkness to light without the whole body, so too the instrument of knowledge can only by the movement of the whole soul be turned from the world of becoming into that of being, and learn by degrees to endure the sight of being, and of the brightest and best of being, or in other words, of the good.

DISCUSSION

The environment of the cave and the binds which imprison its captives represent the chains of ignorance. In such a state, prisoners see only shadows and mistake them for the truth. The release from these chains and the consequent ascent out of the cave is marked by many stages--none of them are easy. Becoming educated and enlightened is a difficult process. Breaking the chains of ignorance is often a painful task. Once out of the cave, the wayfarer again goes through stages of enlightenment--this marks the developmental process each individual will go through in true education. At the end of this process, the enlightened individual feels the moral obligation to return to the setting of the cave to help the other captives to release themselves from the darkness of ignorance. This, too, is no easy task. In fact, it is even sometimes risky. But despite the risk, the truly educated person responds to the duty of all human beings--we are, says Plato, social beings--we need each other even to be ourselves.

After the story, Plato draws some conclusions about the philosophy of education. *Education is not about putting information into empty heads, like sight into blind eyes!* Plato is the father of a theory about the mind known as *rationalism.* This view suggests that the mind is not a blank slate or *tabula rasa.* Rationalism holds that each of us innately possesses understanding, though in an inchoate, undeveloped form. Education is about drawing out from the mind the understanding which is already within us.

Plato's philosophy of education seems to live up to the etymology of the word "educate." It stems from the Latin *educere* which means "to draw out from." To educe is to bring out what is latently there. To educate, then, is to help one develop the potentials and abilities that are present already. It is, as Plato's great teacher Socrates' often put it, like being a midwife--helping to give birth to ideas which are already born in the soul of each and every one of us.

Discussion Questions

1. Can you give examples of how we sometimes get caught up in the "shadows" and "illusions" of life and mistake them for the real thing?

2. Why is each step of the process of leaving the cave marked by pain?

3. Why do you think the prisoners in the cave are so reluctant to listen to the enlightened one who returns?

4. Do you think Plato is right about the nature of the mind? Is the mind, that is, already filled with latent understanding and potential?

5. If you were the released prisoner, would you be so willing to return to the cave and face the difficulties there?

CHAPTER THREE

CONFUCIUS

More than five hundred years before the time of Christ, China gave birth to a man who was to have an enormous influence over that nation and the rest of the world, especially that of eastern Asia. The western world refers to him as Confucius, but this is actually the latinized form of "Kung Fu-Tzu" (Master or Master Teacher). Confucius has been given many venerable titles by the Chinese: "Master Kung, the perfect teacher of antiquity," and "Master Teacher for ten thousand generations," are among the most widely used. For nearly twenty five hundred years Confucius has been a driving force in the politics, religion, and more importantly for our purposes, the system of education in China. In the twentieth century, one of every five persons live in China. It will do us well, therefore, to examine the life and ideas of this great teacher.

Confucius was born in 551 B.C., the son of a family with an aristocratic past. His family had lost much of its status and wealth during a period of political upheaval in China. His father died not long after his birth, but Confucius' mother was diligent in her desire to provide a sound education for him. He was well trained, therefore, in the great classics of Chinese literature as well as in history, poetry, music and archery. Poetry and music were to have a special influence on him, and in the *Analects* (considered to be the most authentic writings concerning the actual teachings of Confucius) the mature Confucius says, "A man's character is formed by the Odes, developed by the Rites . . . and perfected by music." The *Analects* also reveal that at the age of fifteen he set himself the goal of becoming a scholar and teacher. However, as a young boy, Confucius was no bookwormish recluse. He lived a healthy, active life and enjoyed fishing, chariot driving and archery as prized pastimes.

In his late teens Confucius seems to have occupied a minor post in government. Later he began a marriage which was to be unsuccessful and ended in divorce. One son was born to him at this time. In his twenties his loving mother died and true to Chinese tradition, Confucius mourned her for three years by retiring from public life. Chinese tradition teaches that he sought a political career later in life. One legend has Confucius rule as Prime Minister. During his reign, we are told, society ran very smoothly and the crime rate dropped substantially through Confucius' principle of rule by good example rather than strong fisted force. We also learn that his enemies conspired against him and, having somehow lost face, Confucius was forced out. Though he held some minor posts later, he was never again to have a significant post in government for the rest of his life.

Confucius began his career in teaching at the age of twenty two. Tradition tells us that he used his own house as a school and charged small fees for his students whom he would instruct in his favorite subjects; history, poetry, government, morality and music. He taught the art of thinking through conversation with his students about their own opinions on important matters, much in the style of Socrates. Beginning with just a few students, Confucius was rapidly becoming known as a great teacher. He responded to this reputation with authentic humility when he says in the *Analects* that "I am a transmitter and not a creator. I believe in and have a passion for the Ancients." By this Confucius meant that he was devoted to the great ideas already present in China. China did already have a rich intellectual, spiritual and artistic heritage passed on in such classics as the very ancient book of wisdom known as the *I Ching*. But Confucius may have been too humble. He seems to have had an incredible ability to inspire others to see the truths of the great ideas. He loved learning and he sought out pupils who shared this love. Soon he was mentor to more than three thousand, some of whom seemed to follow him as a guru in the religious sense.

Confucius was driven by a central theme and motivating passion. He was deeply convinced that learning and morality were inseparable. Education, he felt, improved the moral character of a person as well as the intellect. We read in the *Analects* that "It is not easy to find a man who has learned for these years without coming to be good." He was convinced that all persons have an innate tendency for goodness, but that a bad education and a bad society can endanger this goodness and shrivel it up. Morality needs good education, and a good education is one based on the moral principles. This point is best illustrated in Confucius' analogy of the tree of virtue as interpreted and discussed by Confucian scholars (for example, Y.C. Yang). For a tree, like a person, has an innate potentiality for growth and development but it needs a proper soil and environment or it will die. In the analogy Confucius illustrates the great "five cardinal virtues" in the following way: *Jen* (the root of the tree) refers to altruism, or the desire for the good of others over and above our own selfish needs and wants. The teaching here, therefore, is that society and education in particular, must be rooted properly, i.e., rooted in the soil of compassion and care for others. *Yi* (the tree's trunk) stands for just righteousness. The trunk of a healthy tree is strong. The strength of the trunk, likewise, depends on a healthy root system. And so we are taught the interdependence of the virtues on each other. *Li* (the branches of the tree), is one of the most important virtues for Confucius. It stands for right and proper actions towards others. The branches of a healthy tree <u>reach out</u>. *Li* is the capacity to reach out to others in good behavior towards them. Again, none of the virtues can operate totally independently. Good branches depend on a strong trunk, just as a strong trunk needs a healthy root system. *Zhi* (the tree's flower) refers to the virtue of wisdom. Wisdom, then, is the flowering of good actions, a strong character and a love for others. A wise person, therefore, does not sit on a mountain top apart from the people in the real world. The wise person interacts with others and is greatly devoted to the <u>practice</u> of morality (this is Confucius' version of "practice rather than preach"). Finally, there is *Xin* (the flower's fruit) which points to the virtue of faithfulness. The faithful person is the fruit born by a society properly rooted. The proper environment allows the roots to take hold; a good society is one which fosters altruism and therefore strengthens the character, improves moral behavior and fosters wisdom and fidelity.

For Confucius, the virtues are all interrelated because the human being is an interrelational creature. We are <u>social</u> creatures. We therefore need society to be truly ourselves; to be truly <u>human</u> persons. Education is central to building a strong society. This must be done from the bottom up, not from the top down. This point is best illustrated in the Confucian text *The Great Learning*, where we read of those societies which prospered that "Their knowledge being complete, their thoughts were sincere. Their thoughts being sincere, their hearts were then rectified. Their hearts being rectified, their persons were cultivated. Their persons being cultivated, their families were regulated. Their families being regulated, their states were rightly governed. Their states being rightly governed, the whole kingdom was made tranquil and happy." The Confucian teaching, therefore, concerning the relationship between society and education, is very strong. Society must support proper education because proper education develops good citizens who, in turn, build and interact with a proper society. Here we find a clear sense of the reciprocity between societal and individual needs.

Largely because of Confucius, China went on to develop and to foster an enthusiastic admiration for learning. After his death in 479 B.C., Confucius' followers mourned him greatly. Some of the faithful, legend teaches, built huts by the grave site and lived in mourning for three years! Soon some seventy Confucian scholars and teachers scattered throughout China and spread the ideas of Confucianism. This was met with periods of failure as well as success. During some dynasties, for example, Confucian ideas were seen as politically threatening. This anti-Confucianism culminated in the execution of many Confucian scholars (some were even buried alive) and the burning of Confucian texts. But this negative reaction was to be only temporary; it ended during the reign of some of the great emperors of the Han dynasty. In 136 B.C., Confucianism became the officially recognized and formal system of education in all of China. Soon there were temples built in Confucius' honor which bore a likeness of him. By the sixth century, every prefecture in China had such a temple erected. This probably contributed to the growing spread of Confucianism as a religion in China as well. In later centuries, the statues were removed and replaced with tablets bearing some of the great teachings of Confucius. This change, no doubt, accurately reflected Confucius' desires to be seen as a transmitter of important truths. It is the teachings and not the man himself which is important.

During our own century, Confucius has survived some formidable attacks. After 1949 and the Marxist revolution led by Mao Tse-tung, the country was forced to turn away from the "old" ideas of philosophy and religion. Confucianism was seen as a non-progressive relic of an overthrown and oppressive past. But since Mao's death in 1977, and the growing relationship and openness to the western world, China has once again turned to the ancient wisdom of Confucius the "Master Teacher." The reading which follows penetrates the ideas of Confucius concerning education.

CONFUCIUS, THE MASTER TEACHER*

The Great Learning

The Text of Confucius:

1. What the Great Learning teaches, is--to illustrate illustrious virtue; to renovate the people; and to rest in the highest excellence.

3. Things have their root and their branches. Affairs have their end and their beginning. To know what is first and what is last will lead near to what is taught in the *Great Learning*.

4. The ancients who wished to illustrate illustrious virtue throughout the kingdom, first ordered well their own States. Wishing to order well their States, they first regulated their families. Wishing to regulate their families, they first cultivated their persons. Wishing to cultivate their persons, they first rectified their hearts. Wishing to rectify their hearts, they first sought to be sincere in their thoughts. Wishing to be sincere in their thoughts, they first extended to the utmost their knowledge. Such extension of knowledge lay in the investigation of things.

5. Things being investigated, knowledge became complete. Their knowledge being complete, their thoughts were sincere. Their thoughts being sincere, their hearts were then rectified. Their hearts being rectified, their persons were cultivated. Their persons being cultivated, their families were regulated. Their families being regulated, their States were rightly

---

* **Source**: **The Four Books**, ed., trans., James Legge, in *The Chinese Classics*, Vol. I (Oxford: Clarendon, 1893).

governed. Their States being rightly governed, the whole kingdom was made tranquil and happy.

6. From the Son of Heaven down to the mass of the people, all must consider the cultivation of the person the root of *everything besides.*

7. It cannot be, when the root is neglected, that what should spring from it will be well ordered. It never has been the case that what was of great importance has been slightly cared for, and, at the same time, that what was of slight importance has been greatly cared for.

Commentary of the philosopher Tsang

Chapter VII:
1. What is meant by, 'The cultivation of the person depends on rectifying the mind,' *may be thus illustrated:*--If a man be under the influence of passion, he will be incorrect in his conduct. He will be the same, if he is under the influence of terror, or under the influence of fond regard, or under that of sorrow and distress.

2. When the mind is not present, we look and do not see; we hear and do not understand; we eat and do not know the taste of what we eat.

3. This is what is meant by saying that the cultivation of the person depends on the rectifying of the mind.

Confucian Analects:

2:11 The Master said, 'If a man keeps cherishing his old knowledge, so as continually to be acquiring new, he may be a teacher of others.'

2:15 The Master said, 'Learning without thought is labour lost; thought without learning is perilous.'

2:17 The Master said, 'Yu, shall I teach you what knowledge is? When you know a thing, to hold that you know it; and when you do not know a thing, to allow that you do not know it;--this is knowledge.'

4:16 The Master said, 'The mind of the superior man is conversant with righteousness; the mind of the mean man is conversant with gain.'

4:17 The Master said, 'When we see men of worth, we should think of equalling them; when we see men of a contrary character, we should turn inwards and examine ourselves.'

5:27 The Master said, 'In a hamlet of ten families, there may be found one honourable and sincere as I am, but not so fond of learning.'

7:1 The Master said, '[I am a] transmitter and not a maker, believing in and loving the ancients . . . .'

7:2 The Master said, 'The silent treasuring up of knowledge; learning without satiety; and instructing others without being wearied:--which one of these things belongs to me?'

7:3 The Master said, 'The leaving virtue without proper cultivation; the not thoroughly discussing what is learned; not being able to move towards righteousness of which a knowledge is gained; and not being able to change what is not good:--these are the things which occasion me solitude.'

7:8 The Master said, 'I do not open up the truth to one who is not eager *to get knowledge*, nor help out any one who is not anxious to explain himself. When I have presented one corner of a subject to anyone, and he cannot from it learn the other three, I do not repeat my lesson.'

7:19 The Master said, 'I am not one who was born in the possession of knowledge; I am one who is fond of antiquity, and earnest in seeking it *there*.'

7:21 The Master said, 'When I walk along with two others, they may serve me as my teachers. I will select their good qualities and follow them, their bad qualities and avoid them.'

7:24 There were four things which the Master taught,--letters, ethics, devotion of soul, and truthfulness.

9:4 There were four things from which the Master was entirely free. He had no foregone conclusions, no arbitrary predeterminations, no obstinacy, and no egoism.

9:7 The Master said, 'Am I indeed possessed of knowledge? I am not knowing. But if a mean person, who appears quite empty-like, ask anything of me, I set it forth from one end to the other, and exhaust it.'

12:16 The Master said, 'The superior man *seeks to* perfect the admirable qualities of men, and does not *seek to* perfect their bad qualities. The mean man does the opposite of this.'

15:23 Tsze-kung asked, saying, 'Is there one word which may serve as a rule of practice for all one's life?' The Master said, 'Is not RECIPROCITY such a word? What you do not want done to yourself, do not do to others.'

17:2 The Master said, 'By nature, men are nearly alike; by practice, they get to be wide apart.'

17:3 The Master said, 'There are only the wise of the highest class, and the stupid of the lowest class, who cannot be changed.'

The   Doctrine   of   the   Mean

1:4 While there are no stirrings of pleasure, anger, sorrow, or joy, the mind may be said to be in the state of EQUILIBRIUM. When those feelings have been stirred, and they act in their due degree, there ensues what may be called the state of HARMONY. This EQUILIBRIUM is the great root *from which grow all the human actings* in the world, and this HARMONY is the universal path *which they all should pursue.*

1:5 Let the states of equilibrium and harmony exist in perfection, and a happy order will prevail throughout heaven and earth, and all things will be nourished and flourish.

2:3 The Master said, 'Perfect is the virtue which is according to the Mean! Rare have they long been among the people, who could practice it!'

8:3 [The Master said] 'When one cultivates to the utmost the principles of his nature, and exercises them on the principle of reciprocity, he is not far from the path. What you do not like done to yourself, do not do to others.'

15:5 The Master said, 'In archery we have something like the way of the superior man. When the archer misses the centre of the target, he turns round and seeks the cause of his failure in himself.'

20:11 [The Master said] 'He who knows these three things [knowledge, magnanimity, and energy], knows how to cultivate his own character. Knowing how to cultivate his own character, he knows how to govern other men. Knowing how to govern other men, he knows how to govern the kingdom with all its States and families.'

21:21 [The Master said] 'When we have intelligence resulting from sincerity, this condition is to be ascribed to nature; when we have sincerity resulting from intelligence, this condition is to be ascribed to instruction. But given the sincerity, and there shall be intelligence; given the intelligence, and their shall be the sincerity.'

25:1 Sincerity is that whereby self-completion is effected and its way is that by which man must direct himself.

25:2 Sincerity is the end and beginning of things; without sincerity there would be nothing. On this account, the superior man regards the attainment of sincerity as the most excellent thing.

25:3 The possessor of sincerity does not merely accomplish the self-completion of himself. With this quality he completes *other men and* things *also.* The completing himself *shows his* perfect virtue. The completing *other men* and things *shows his* knowledge.

DISCUSSION

With these famous teachings from Confucius and Confucianism, we gain some insight into the major points of focus that this great thinker emphasized. It is clear above all else that the major goal of true education, for the Confucian, is the *cultivation of character*. As *The Great Learning* teaches, this is "the root of everything besides." And this is no selfish or individual goal either. In cultivating ourselves, that is, we do indeed achieve the "self-completion" spoken of in *The Doctrine of the Mean*. This is the Confucian equivalent to Aristotle's fulfilled or happy person, and to Maslow's "self-actualizing" person. But the self is no isolated ego, as far as Confucianism is concerned. The self is always related to others. And as the last line quoted from this work says, the self-completed person "completes other men" also. So the goal is to cultivate not just the individual, but to cultivate society as a whole.

And how do we cultivate the person and society? For Confucius, it all hinges on sound education and knowledge. His clear teaching is that good education elicits knowledge, which makes our thoughts sincere, which rectifies our hearts and cultivates our persons. "The cultivation of the person" we are told, "depends on the rectifying of the mind."

What would be some of the characteristics of good education for Confucius? First, we must build upon the wisdom of the past. Confucius' love for the ancient wisdom is often repeated. Teachers are to be "transmitters" of knowledge. But what is knowledge? Confucius' answer is very much in the tradition of Socrates who taught that "knowledge is virtue." At least in part, Socrates here means that true knowledge is akin to the virtue of humility: knowing that you do not know everything! And so, Confucius' words ring true: "When you know a thing, to hold that you know it; and when you do not know a thing, to allow that you do not know it;--this is knowledge." But as *The Doctrine of the Mean* teaches, along with knowledge, we must pursue magnanimity and energy. Such goals involve the state of *harmony* and *equilibrium*.

In the end, we find these qualities by searching within ourselves. And so Confucius teaches us to "turn inwards and examine ourselves." Again, the comparison with Socrates is striking, for it was Socrates' who taught us to "Know thyself."

Discussion   Questions

1. Do you agree with Confucius that the major goal of education is the cultivation of a person's character?

2. If you do agree with the above, do you think that present education achieves this goal? Does it <u>seek</u> this goal?

3. Do you agree that learning somehow inspires goodness within our characters, as Confucius seems to have believed? Does education always lead to goodness?

4. Confucius teaches that human beings are fundamentally social creatures or interrelational. Do you agree?

5. Should a major goal of education be the concern for strengthening our social bonds? Does present education do this? What are some of the ways it could be changed to do this if it is not already?

CHAPTER FOUR

JOHN LOCKE

In our discussion of Plato, we were introduced to the theory about the mind known as *rationalism.* This is the view that the mind, at birth, is already in possession of some innate ideas or truths. Life is a process, according to this theory, of building upon these innate understandings by drawing out or *educing* other truths which we "have" inchoately in our minds

When we turn to the British philosopher John Locke (1632-1704), we examine one of the founders of a view which rejects the major assumptions found in rationalism. Locke's view is referred to as *empiricism*, and dates back at least as far as Aristotle (Plato's great pupil: 384-322 B.C.) who said of the mind that it was "like a writing tablet upon which nothing stands written." This view has come to be known as the *tabula rasa* (empty tablet) theory. Locke, in his monumental two volume work, *An Essay Concerning Human Understanding*, suggests that we "suppose the mind to be, as we say, white paper, void of all characters, without any ideas . . . ." In saying this, Locke clearly declares himself an empiricist, and raises as well some obvious questions: where does, then, our knowledge of ideas come from? How do we gain truth and understanding, if we begin with blank slates?

These questions are of fundamental importance to the study of education. For how can we set about educating minds if we do not already know what the mind is like, and by what means it comes to know things? Locke believed that too many philosophers before him had made all sorts of dogmatic claims about various truths the human mind is able to know (about the nature of the world, for example, or even about God) without analyzing very carefully the nature of the mind itself. He became convinced that unless we investigate the instrument itself, we can be certain neither of the *kinds* of truths the mind can know, nor the best *ways* the mind can come to know them.

In choosing the *tabula rasa* view, Locke speaks to the *kind* of tool the mind is. What, then, about the *how*? By what means, that is, or by what avenues, does the mind become filled with ideas? Locke's answer is unequivocal: "To this I answer, in one word, from EXPERIENCE. In that all our knowledge is founded; and from that it ultimately derives itself." Here we gain insight into why this view that Locke and others accept is referred to as "empiricism" (*empeiria* = Gk: experience).

Locke was a noted physician of his day. No doubt, his experiences with the science of medicine informed his views about how knowledge is gained. It is clear, also, that his profession influenced his view about the kind of knowledge the mind is best suited for. He was, that is, less sure about attaining absolute, certain truth than were the rationalists before him (especially Rene Descartes: 1596-1650). You cannot wait and argue about certainty before you treat the patient. You must operate, lest the patient die. In doing so, you do what you can, guided by the successful experiences of scientists before you. Learning is experience and experience is learning. What we learn is often more probable than certain.

But if the mind is empty from the start, how can it learn anything from experience at all? If it is totally blank, like "white paper", would not knowledge be impossible? Taken literally, if this were a complete description of its make-up, the mind would, it seems, remain forever unable to be informed by experience. But the empiricists view the mind as being "impressed" by experience, just as, in the most often used analogy, a piece of wax is impressed with the characters on a signet ring when the two are brought together. But wax is not "nothing". Wax has specific characteristics which allow it to "receive" the information from this experience. So too, the mind, in order to be able to "receive" ideas from experience in general, cannot simply be a blank, empty "nothing."

A closer reading of Locke reveals that though the empiricist rejects innate truths already present in the mind, he does not reject "natural" faculties, tendencies, and capacities of the mind. Locke was well aware that we do not enter this world without latent characteristics and potentialities. But experience is what fills the mind with ideas. As he explains, the "senses at first let in *particular* ideas, and furnish the yet empty cabinet." We can assume, therefore, that by "empty" Locke here means empty of content (ideas), and not empty of structure or capacity.

Having thus defined the mind and the way in which it becomes informed, we can now proceed to the question of how to educate young minds. Since experience is the source of all knowledge, what sorts of experiences should we promote (for not all experiences are equal nor good)? How can we best "shape" the young mind? What should be our method of education?

The reading which follows is excerpted from Locke's essay "Some Thoughts Concerning Education." As the title suggests, it is not meant to be a final and complete philosophy of education. Locke offers it rather as a good start, with the intention of providing advice for us all (especially parents and teachers). He focuses more on where we should start and the attitudes we should take, as well as the assumptions we should and should not make. In particular, Locke says some very interesting things about punishment and conformity, and the integrity and inventiveness of young minds. Most importantly, he speaks to the development of good habits in learning. In Locke's day, the popular method of teaching was that of instilling fear in the child, especially seeking as a goal the rote memorization of many rules and other kinds of information which could be regurgitated on exams or in the presence of one's peers and before the ominous presence of one's "teacher." Locke speaks of the failures and inadequacies of this method. He offers instead some ideas which he believes will promote "true education."

Locke's ideas are clearly influenced by his own personal experiences. He was, like many scholars before him, critical of the standard practice of educating children. Of his own education, Locke once complained that he was "perplexed with obscure terms and useless questions." The reading makes aware the need for teachers who can dispel obscurity and uselessness. The child's mind is young. It is not prepared for deep, profound, and penetrating ideas right away. And the way in which the teacher can teach ideas to the child is by indicating the usefulness of them. Children naturally desire the useful things in life. They also are naturally inclined towards the playful atmosphere. Locke had a very modern sense of the need for making learning playful and akin to recreation, rather than worklike and tedious.

Finally, he addresses the issue of priorities in education. The reader may be surprised to find that Locke does not place learning first on a scale of things he deems necessary for our children. It is more important that we seek to instill good characters in our children (especially by promoting virtue, wisdom and breeding), for a bad character can be made worse not better by education. In the following, these and other ideas are discussed in detail.

LOCKE ON DEVELOPING GOOD HABITS*

. . . 1. A sound mind in a sound body, is a short but full description of a happy state in this world: he that has these two, has little more to wish for; and he that wants either of them, will be but little the better for anything else. Men's happiness or misery is [for the] most part of their own making. . . . and I think I may say, that, of all the men we meet with, nine parts of ten are what they are, good or evil, useful or not, by their education. It is that which makes the great difference in mankind. The little, or almost insensible, impressions on our tender infancies, have very important and lasting consequences . . . .

32. . . . [W]e have reason to conclude, that great care is to be had of the forming children's minds, and giving them that seasoning early, which shall influence their lives always after . . . .

33. As the strength of the body lies chiefly in being able to endure hardships, so also does that of the mind. And the great principle and foundation of all virtue and worth is placed in this, that a man is able to deny himself his own desires, cross his own inclinations, and purely follow what reason directs as best, though the appetite lean the other way.

34. The great mistake I have observed in people's breeding their children has been, that this has not been taken care enough of in its due season; that the mind has not been made obedient to discipline, and pliant to reason, when first it was most tender, most easy to be bowed . . . .

---

* Source: John Locke, "Some Thoughts Concerning Education", in *Works of John Locke* (London: Thomas Tegg, et al., Vol. IX, 1823).

38.   It seems plain to me, that the principle of all virtue and excellency lies in a power of denying ourselves the satisfaction of our own desires, where reason does not authorize them. This power is to be got and improved by custom, made easy and familiar by an early practice . . . .

39.   I say not this as if children were not to be indulged in anything, or that I expected they should, in hanging-sleeves, have the reason and conduct of counsellors. I consider them as children, who must be tenderly used, who must play, and have play things. . . . I have seen children at a table, who, whatever was there, never asked for any thing, but contentedly took what was given them: and at another place I have seen others cry for everything they saw, must be served out of every dish, and that first too. What made this vast difference but this, that one was accustomed to have what they called or cried for, the other to go without it? The younger they are, the less, I think, are their unruly and disorderly appetites to be complied with . . . .

40.   Those therefore that intend ever to govern their children, should begin it whilst they are very little; and look that they perfectly comply with the will of their parents . . . .

42.   Thus much for the setting your authority over children in general. Fear and awe ought to give you the first power over their minds, and love and friendship in riper years to hold it: for the time must come, when they will be past the rod and correction . . . . Every man must some time or other be trusted to himself, and his own conduct; and he that is a good, a virtuous, and able man, must be made so within. And therefore, what he is to receive from education, what is to sway and influence his life, must be something put into him betimes: habits woven into the very principles of his nature; and not a counterfeit carriage, and dissembled outside, put on by fear, only to avoid the present anger of a father, who perhaps may disinherit him.

43. . . . But . . . I am very apt to think, that great severity of punishment does but very little good; nay, great harm in education: and I believe it will be found, that, *caeteris paribus*, those children who have been most chastised, seldom make the best men. All that I have contended for, is, that whatsoever rigour is necessary, it is more to be used, the younger children are; and, having by a due application wrought its effect, it is to be relaxed, and changed into a milder sort of government . . . .

46. . . . [I]f the mind be curbed, and humbled too much in children; if their spirits be abased and broken much, by too strict an hand over them; they lose all their vigour and industry, and are in a worse state than the former . . . .

47. The usual lazy and short way by chastisement, and the rod, which is the only instrument of government that tutors generally know, or ever think of, is the most unfit of any to be used in education; because it tends to both those mischiefs; . . . the Scylla and Charybdis, which, on the one hand or the other, ruin all that miscarry.

48. 1. This kind of punishment contributes not at all to the mastery of our natural propensity to indulge corporal and present pleasure and to avoid pain at any rate; but rather encourages it; and thereby strengthens that in us, which is the root, from whence spring all vicious actions and the irregularities of life . . . .

49. 2. This sort of correction naturally breeds an aversion to that which it is the tutor's business to create a liking to. How obvious is it to observe, that children come to hate things which were at first acceptable to them, when they find themselves whipped, and chid, and teazed about them? . . .

51. 4. If severity carried to the highest pitch does prevail, and works a cure upon the present unruly distemper, it is often bringing in the room of it a worse and more

dangerous disease, by breaking the mind; and then, in the place of a disorderly young fellow, you have a low-spirited moped creature: who, however with his unnatural sobriety he may please silly people, who commend tame inactive children, because they make no noise, nor give them any trouble; yet, at last, will probably prove as uncomfortable a thing to his friends, as he will be, all his life, an useless thing to himself and others.

52. Beating then, and all other sorts of slavish and corporal punishments, are not the discipline fit to be used in the education of those who would have wise, good, and ingenuous men; and therefore very rarely to be applied, and that only on great occasions, and cases of extremity . . . .

54. But if you take away the rod . . . how then (will you say) shall children be governed? . . . I advise their parents and governors always to carry this in their minds, that children are to be treated as rational creatures . . . .

56. The rewards and punishments then whereby we should keep children in order are quite of another kind; and of that force, that when we can get them once to work, the business, I think, is done, and the difficulty is over. Esteem and disgrace are, of all others, the most powerful incentives to the mind, when once it is brought to relish them. If you can once get into children a love of credit, and an apprehension of shame and disgrace, you have put into them the true principle, which will constantly work, and incline them to the right. But, it will be asked, How shall this be done?

I confess, it does not, at first appearance, want some difficulty; but yet I think it worth our while to seek the ways (and practise them when found) to attain this, which I look on as the great secret of education . . . .

63. But if a right course be taken with children, there will not be so much need of the application of the common

reward and punishments, as we imagined, and as the general practice has established. For all their innocent folly, playing, and childish actions, are to be left perfectly free and unrestrained, as far as they can consist with the respect due to those that are present; and that with the greatest allowance. . . . [T]his gamesome humour, which is wisely adapted by nature to their age and temper, should rather be encouraged, to keep up their spirits, and improve their strength and health, than curbed or restrained: and the chief art is to make all that they have to do, sport and play too.

64. And here give me leave to take notice of one thing I think a fault in the ordinary method of education; and that is, the charging of children's memories, upon all occasions, with rules and precepts, which they often do not understand, and are constantly as soon as forgot as given. If it be some action you would have done, or done otherwise; whenever they forget, or do it awkwardly, make them do it over and over again, til they are perfect: whereby you will get these two advantages: first, to see whether it be an action they can do, or is fit to be expected of them. For sometimes children are bid to do things, which, upon trial, they are found not able to do; and had need be taught and exercised in, before they are required to do them. But it is much easier for a tutor to command, than to teach. Secondly, another thing got by it will be this, that by repeating the same action, till it be grown habitual in them, the performance will not depend on memory, or reflection, the concomitant of prudence and age, and not of childhood; but will be natural in them. . . . Having this way cured in your child any fault, it is cured for ever: and thus, one by one, you may weed them out all, and plant habits you please.

65. I have seen parents so heap rules on their children, that it was impossible for the poor little ones to remember a tenth part of them, much less to observe them. However, they were either by words or blows corrected for the breach of those multiplied and often very impertinent precepts . . . .

66.   But   pray   remember,   children   are   not   to   be   taught   by rules,   which   will   always   be   sipping   out   of   their   memories. What   you   think   necessary   for   them   to   do,   settle   in   them   by   an indispensable   practice,   as   often   as   the   occasion   returns;   and,   if it   be   possible,   make   occasions.   This   will   beget   habits   in   them, which,   being   once   established,   operate   of   themselves   easily   and naturally,   without   the   assistance   of   memory . . . .   By   this method   we   shall   see,   whether   what   is   required   of   him   be adapted   to   his   capacity,   and   any   way   suited   to   the   child's natural   genius   and   constitution: for   that   too   must   be   considered in   a   right   education.   We   must   not   hope   wholly   to   change   their original   tempers,   nor   make   the   gay   pensive   and   grave,   nor   the melancholy   sportive,   without   spoiling   them.   God   has   stamped certain   characters   upon   men's   minds,   which,   like   their   shapes, may   perhaps   be   a   little   mended;   but   can   hardly   be   totally altered   and   transformed   into   the   contrary.

. . .   For,   in   many   cases,   all   that   we   can   do,   or   should   aim at,   is,   to   make   the   best   of   what   nature   has   given;   to   prevent   the vices   and   faults   to   which   a   constitution   is   most   inclined,   and give   it   all   the   advantages   it   is   capable   of.   Every   one's   natural genius   should   be   carried   as   far   as   it   could;   but   to   attempt   the putting   another   upon   him;   will   be   but   labour   in   vain;   and   what is   so   plaistered   on   will   at   best   sit   but   untowardly,   and   have always   hanging   to   it   the   ungracefulness   of   constraint   and affectation . . . .

73.   None   of   these   things   they   are   to   learn   should   ever   be made   a   burden   to   them,   or   imposed   on   them   as   a   task. Whatever   is   so   proposed   presently   becomes   irksome: the   mind takes   an   aversion   to   it,   though   before   it   were   a   thing   of   delight or   indifferency.   Let   a   child   be   but   ordered   to   whip   his   top   at   a certain   time   every   day,   whether   he   has   or   has   not   a   mind   to   it; let   this   be   but   required   of   him   as   a   duty . . .   and   see   whether he   will   not   soon   be   weary   of   any   play   at   this   rate.   Is   it   not   so with   grown   men?   What   they   do   cheerfully   of   themselves,   do they   not   presently   grow   sick   of,   and   can   no   more   endure,   as soon   as   they   find   it   is   expected   of   them   as   a   duty?   Children

have as much a mind to show that they are free that their own good actions come from themselves. that they are absolute and independent, as any of the proudest of you grown men, think of them as you please . . . .

81. It will perhaps be wondered, that I mention reasoning with children: and yet I cannot but think that the true way of dealing with them. They understand it as early as they do language; and, if I misobserve not, they love to be treated as rational creatures sooner than is imagined. It is a pride should be cherished in them, and, as much as can be, made the greatest instrument to turn them by.

But when I talk of reasoning, I do not intend any other but such as is suited to the child's capacity and apprehension . . . .

95. . . . [A] father will do well, as his son grows up, and is capable of it, to talk familiarly with him; nay, ask his advice, and consult with him, about those things which he has any knowledge or understanding. By this the father . . . will put serious considerations into his son's thoughts, better than any rules or advices he can give him. The sooner you teat him as a man, the sooner he will begin to be one . . . .

118. Curiosity in children . . . is but an appetite after knowledge, and therefore ought to be encouraged in them, not only as a good sign, but as the great instrument nature has provided, to remove that ignorance they were born with, and which without this busy inquisitiveness will make them dull and useless creatures . . . And I doubt not but one great reason, why many children abandon themselves wholly to silly sports, and trifle away all their time insipidly, is, because they have found their curiosity baulked, and their inquiries neglected. But had they been treated with more kindness and respect, and their questions answered, as they should, to their satisfaction, I doubt not but they would have taken more pleasure in learning, and improving their knowledge, wherein

there would be still newness and variety, which is what they are delighted with, than in returning over and over to the same play and play things . . . .

134. That which every gentleman (that takes any care of his education) desires for his son, besides the estate he leaves him, is contained (I suppose) in these four things, virtue, wisdom, breeding, and learning . . . .

135. I place virtue as the first and most necessary of these endowments that belong to a man or a gentleman, as absolutely requisite to make him valued and beloved by others, acceptable or tolerable to himself. Without that, I think, he will be happy neither in this, nor the other world . . . .

140. Wisdom I take, in the popular acceptation, for a man's managing his business ably, and with foresight, in this world . . . . To accustom a child to have true notions of things, and not be satisfied till he has them; to raise his mind to great and worthy thoughts; and to keep him at a distance from falsehood, and cunning, which has always a broad mixture of falsehood in it; is the fittest preparation of a child for wisdom . . . .

141. The next good quality belonging to a gentleman, is good-breeding. There are two sorts of ill-breeding: the one, a sheepish bashfulness; and the other, a misbecoming negligence and disrespect in our carriage; both which are avoided, by duly observing this one rule, Not to think meanly of ourselves, and not to think meanly of others . . . .

147. You will wonder, perhaps, that I put learning last, especially if I tell you I think it the least part. This may seem strange in the mouth of a bookish man. . . . Reading, and writing, and learning, I allow to be necessary, but yet not the chief business. I imagine you would think him a very foolish fellow, that should not value a virtuous, or a wise man, infinitely before a great scholar. Not but that I think learning a

great help to both, in well disposed minds; but yet it must be confessed also, that in others not so disposed, it helps them only to be more foolish, or worse men . . . .

150. [M]asters and teachers should raise no difficulties to their scholars; but, on the contrary, should smooth their way . . . . Keep the mind in an easy calm temper, when you would have it receive your instructions, or any increase of knowledge. It is as impossible to draw fair and regular characters on a trembling mind, as on a shaking paper.

The great skill of a teacher is to get and keep the attention of his scholar: whilst he has that, he is sure to advance as fast as the learner's abilities will carry him . . . .

177. [U]nder whose care soever a child is put to be taught, during the tender and flexible years of his life, this is certain, it should be one who thinks Latin and language the least part of education; one, who knowing how much virtue, and well-tempered soul, is to be preferred to any sort of learning or language, makes it his chief business to form the mind of his scholars, and give that a right disposition: which, if once got, though all the rest should be neglected, would, in due time, produce all the rest; and which if it be not got, and settled, so as to keep out ill and vicious habits, languages and sciences, and all the other accomplishments of education, will be to no purpose, but to make the worse or more dangerous man . . . .

DISCUSSION

Education is, says Locke, "that which makes the great difference." Whether we are "good or evil, useful or not," depends for the most part on the quality of care we give to our children. Throughout, Locke refers to the duties of parents as well as teachers. Education, in the wider sense in which he is taking it, includes the entire environment surrounding the child. Locke is speaking, therefore, to all who have relationships with children--parents, teachers, and society in general--we are all "teachers" in this sense.

What is Locke's advice to us? We are not to indulge the desires of children or they will never learn the internal mastery of these by the reason, which is the mark of a self-controlled, useful citizen. On the other hand, we will fail miserably if we counter unruly tendencies with severe punishments. Such external punishment will produce either robotic automotons, operating only on the principles of pleasure and pain, or broken spirits who become no good to themselves nor to anyone else. Locke offers in the place of external punishment, the internal mechanism of self-esteem. How can we foster self-esteem? He recognizes that this may not be easy. But discovering the answer to this question will reveal "the great secret of education." What Locke gives us is a set of guidelines for bringing this about.

First, we must call to our aid the great teacher of habit. In so doing, we must practice the habits we preach. The child very keenly aware of the meaning of hypocrisy long before he can say the word or spell it! We must all be good examples to children. Also, we must acknowledge the dignity and worth of the child's own ideas. We need to encourage their questions, no matter how silly they seem to us, we must take them very seriously. We should even, on occasion, seek out advice from the child. This will have important effects on their own picture of themselves as worthwhile. Above all, we need to seek to produce a calm temper (self-confidence) in the child since, as Locke so aptly puts it, "it is as impossible to draw fair and regular characters on a trembling mind, as on a shaky paper."

The key seems to be, the appeal to the natural tendencies of the child. It was Locke's "fancy" as he says, "that learning might be made a play and recreation to children . . . ." The teacher who succeeds in doing this, has learned to become a true teacher indeed.

Discussion   Questions

1 Do you agree with Locke's views about the role of
punishment in education?   Explain where you might disagree
and why.

2. Why is the development of good habits so important,
according to Locke? Do you agree?

3. Locke wants education to be more like play and recreation.
Is this really possible?   Can you think of specific ways of
bringing this about? Explain.

4. Why does Locke place learning last in a set of things
desirable for our children?   Do you agree with his ordering of
these?   Explain how yours would be different.

5. What do you think a Lockean classroom would look like?
What would a Lockean teacher be like?   Explain.

CHAPTER FIVE

JEAN JACQUES ROUSSEAU

Jean Jacques Rousseau (1712-1778) was one of the most influential thinkers the world has ever produced. His life and ideas either directly or indirectly impacted upon the Romantic movement, the French Revolution, the transformation of education and revival of religion in Europe, as well as upon such notable individuals as Hume, Voltaire, Kant and Marx. This is impressive enough, but what makes it all the more remarkable was that it was so unexpected. Rousseau was an unlikely candidate for such an illustrious career. His mother died within a few days after his birth, and his father abandoned him when he was about ten to the care of an aunt. He had, therefore, little formal education (it ended at age twelve). Of his boarding school experience, Rousseau was to later write in his monumental autobiographical *Confessions*, that there "we were to learn . . . all the insignificant trash that has obtained the name of education." These are not exactly the beginnings one would expect of a man who was to become a major force on literature, art, poetry and philosophy. And if his beginnings were an obstacle, the end of his life and career, too, was marked with impediments and personal conflicts. Two of his major works were published in the same year (1762). These were the *Social Contract* (a political treatise) and his *Emile* (a book about educational reform). The ideas found in these famous texts came to be criticized and rejected by the established authorities from both Church and State. Consequently, it became necessary for Rousseau to take refuge, but many states were hostile to him--three had outlawed his ideas and he received a condemnation from the Catholic Church. These real threats to his own personal security were unfortunately mixed with Rousseau's apparently unstable mental condition. He seems to have suffered from severe hypochondria and extreme paranoia. He even suspected some of his closest friends (David Hume, for example) of conspiring against him. At the end of his life, Rousseau had more than his share of real, physical ailments as well.

But Rousseau was from the start a sort of stranger in his own land and time. He lived during the so-called "Enlightenment" period, or "The Age of Reason" in France and in Europe in general. The prominent enlightenment thinkers like Voltaire and Diderot were championing *reason and science* as the true guide for humankind, as a replacement of *faith and religion* which had so dominated the middle ages and part of the renaissance. The enlightenment thinkers were firmly convinced that reason and science could promise humankind progress and even salvation (in the social, political, and economic, if not in the religious sense). But Rousseau was actually out of step with this new movement. He was, in fact, much more of a "Romantic" than an enlightenment thinker. Romanticism, as it became used to describe the artists, poets and literary genius of the century after Rousseau's death, was reliant on *feeling* and *conscience* more so than reason and science. The romantics were critical of some of the consequences of science, and they found in Rousseau a deserving champion. Indeed, Rousseau's first major writing was his prize-winning *Discourse on the Arts and Sciences*, wherein he argued that all the great "progress" supported by the enlightenment, had, in reality, a negative effect on humanity. Science and reason had made humankind worse, not better! This argument was, of course, rejected by the scholars and famed philosophers of the day. And it was rather easy for them to attack the *Discourse*, since, as Rousseau later admitted, it was riddled with historical inaccuracies and weak logic. But Rousseau never abandoned (though he certainly qualified) his attack on the "progress of civilization" touted by the spirit dominant in his age. More clear and understandable was his criticism of society in general, and it is to this that we now turn.

Rousseau taught that human nature was essentially good. He therefore rejected any notion of "original sin" and proposed instead a notion of the human being as a "noble savage." "Man is naturally good", he wrote; our original, natural condition is not to blame for the ills we see in our world. It was mainly, he thought, our social institutions which corrupted our natural impulses and tendencies. How does society corrupt us? There were at least two interconnected answers that Rousseau offered. In the first place, society restrains our freedom: "Man is born free; and everywhere he is in chains." Secondly, society tends to create artificiality and, ultimately, deception: "we no longer dare to seem what we really are, but lie under a perpetual restraint." With these criticisms of society, Rousseau can be seen as the major forerunner of, for example, the warnings from Marx concerning the dangers of certain social structures (for Marx, in particular, of capitalism), and of the existentialist's concern for the loss of individual freedoms and individual authenticity. Society can turn the individual, with all the uniqueness and dignity befitting a true individual, into merely another member of the herd, where individuality becomes lost in the faceless crowd.

What should be done in the face of this threat from society? Rousseau proposed an inward path. The human being will have to go back to the natural source of truth. Rousseau did not mean here a retreat to some "state of nature" outside civilization's grasp. He knew that this would be an impractical idea. However, it was a retreat to an older, more natural state of society that he prized. Rousseau is a major voice proposing the so-called *laissez-faire* kind of society (a "hands-off" policy, united under the motto: "that government governs best which governs least"). But the inward path he suggested was not so much about society. If society was the threat, the solution was not, then, in society either. What Rousseau offered was a return to an innate and trustworthy resource in each and every

individual. This was <u>not</u> another rationalist call to innate ideas.
For Rousseau, the true, innate and natural guide for us is not to
be found in the realm of ideas, but in our innate *feelings*.
Before we have any ideas, he argued, we first have feelings.
And these feelings could be relied upon, for example, as a
source for our conscience and true morality. "What I feel to be
right is right, what I feel to be wrong is wrong," he said.
Feeling was to become for Rousseau so all-encompassing that in
the end he wrote, "to exist is to feel."

Here we see the beginnings of the Romantic movement in
art, poetry and literature. But what can we say about the
consequences for education? Rousseau was very interested in
educational reform. Like Locke before him, he looked upon the
traditional methods as stifling and ineffectual. Although he
himself had very little formal education, he was a very
precocious child. He learned to read very early, and as a young
man he acquainted himself with the classical texts of antiquity
and was familiar with the works of his contemporaries like
Voltaire. But Rousseau knew that formal education was
necessary. And he knew of the need for fundamental changes.
Like Plato, he was also aware that one's view of social
institutions such as education, were in large part dependent on
one's view of human nature. We have already seen some of
Rousseau's philosophy of human nature. What is natural about
our humanness must be sought out and nurtured. But what
kind of creatures are we really? And what kind of society and
education are we best suited for? While we are naturally good,
we are not, realized Rousseau, naturally perfect and fully
adaptable to any society, and we are not veterans at social
behavior. At bottom, thought Rousseau, our fundamental,
natural impulse is "self-love." The human creature naturally
desires, first and foremost, the satisfaction of personal needs.
But this self-love, for Rousseau, should not be confused with
some natural selfishness portrayed, for example, in the egoism
of the British philosopher Thomas Hobbes (1588-1679). In
Hobbes' view, the natural state of humanity (the "state of
nature") quickly becomes a "state of war" because of the

natural selfishness and competition which arises therein. For Rousseau, however, selfishness and competition are not products of nature but of society. In Rousseau's "state of nature," the human being competes with no one else and has no reason to be selfish. It is only when the "noble savage" has entered into social arrangements that competition arises. We must take great care, therefore, to provide a good transition into the social world for the "noble savage" still in the child. Hence, among the first educational reforms Rousseau proposed was his warning not to make it competitive. The competitive atmosphere, he thought, would more often than not produce an artificial result; i.e., the desire to win the teacher's approval in besting one's peers. True education should desire learning not winning, and self-approval (self-esteem) is to be prized over the approval of others.

The attempt, in short, should be to keep education natural, simple, and respectful of individual differences and needs. Children, argued Rousseau, are not peas in a pod. The desire should not, then, be to teach them to think alike. Children are to be taught, primarily, to think for themselves. The reader will recognize these and other ideas in the following portion from Rousseau's *Emile*, about the education of an imaginary young boy.

ROUSSEAU ON KEEPING EDUCATION NATURAL*

Book I

. . . Plants are fashioned by cultivation, men by education. We are born feeble and need strength; possessing nothing, we need assistance; beginning without intelligence, we need judgment. All that we lack at birth and need when grown up is given us by education. This education comes to us from nature, from men, or from things. The internal development of our faculties and organs is the education of nature. The use we learn to make of this development is the education of men. What comes to us from our experience of the things that affect us is the education of things. Each of us therefore is fashioned by three teachers. When their lessons are at variance the pupil is badly educated, and is never at peace with himself. When they coincide and lead to a common goal he goes straight to his mark and lives single-minded. Now, of these three educations the one due to nature is independent of us, and the one from things only depends on us to a limited extent. The education that comes to us from men is the only one within our control, and even that is doubtful. Who can hope to have the entire direction of the words and deeds of all the people around a child?

It is only by good luck that the goal can be reached. What is this goal? It is nature's own goal. Since the three educations must work together for a perfect result, the one that cannot be modified determines the course of the other two . . . .

There would be no difficulty if our three educations were merely different. But what is to be done when they are at

* Source: Jean Jacques Rousseau, **Emile**, in *The Emile of Jean Jacques Rousseau: Selections*, ed. William Boyd (New York: Teachers College Press, 1956). Reprinted by permission.

cross purposes? Consistency is plainly impossible when we seek to educate a man for others, instead of for himself. If we have to combat either nature or society, we must choose between making a man or a citizen. We cannot make both. There is an inevitable conflict of aims, from which come two opposing forms of education: the one communal and public, the other individual and domestic.

To get a good idea of communal education, read Plato's *Republic*. It is not a political treatise, as those who merely judge books by their titles think. It is the finest treatise on education ever written. Communal education in this sense, however, does not and can not now exist . . . .

I do not regard the instruction given in those ridiculous establishments called colleges as "public," any more than the ordinary kind of education . . . .

There remains then domestic education, the education of nature . . . .

A man of high rank once suggested that I should be his son's tutor. But having had experience already I knew myself unfit and I refused. Instead of the difficult task of educating a child, I now undertake the easier task of writing about it. To provide details and examples in illustration of my views and to avoid wandering off into airy speculations, I propose to set forth the education of Emile, an imaginary pupil, from birth to manhood. . . . .

. . . I assume that Emile is no genius, but a boy of ordinary ability: . . . that he is rich, . . . that he is to all intents and purposes an orphan, whose tutor having undertaken the parent's duties will also have their right to control all the circumstances of his upbringing; and, finally, that he is a vigorous, healthy, well-built child . . . .

Book II

. . . The more children can do for themselves the less help they need from other people. Added strength brings with it the same sense needed for its direction. With the coming of self-consciousness at this second stage individual life really begins. Memory extends the sense of identity over all the moment's of the child's existence. He becomes one and the same person, capable of happiness or sorrow. From this point on it is essential to regard him as a moral being. . . .

Your first duty is to be humane. Love childhood. Look with friendly eyes on its games, its pleasures, its amiable dispositions. Which of you does not sometimes look back regretfully on the age when laughter was ever on the lips and the heart free of care? Why steal from the little innocents the enjoyment of a time that passes all too quickly? . . .

If we are to keep in touch with reality we must never forget what befits our condition. Humanity has its place in the scheme of things. Childhood has its place in the scheme of human life. We must view the man as a man, and the child as a child. The best way to ensure human well-being is to give each person his place in life and keep him there, regulating the passions in accordance with the individual constitution. The rest depends on external factors without our control. . . .

There are two kinds of dependence: dependence on things, which is natural, and dependence on men, which is social. . . .

Keep the child in sole dependence on things and you will follow the natural order in the course of his education. . . .

Excessive severity and excessive indulgence are equally to be avoided. If you let children suffer you endanger health and life. If you are over-careful in shielding them from trouble of every kind you are laying up much unhappiness for the future . . . .

"Reason with children" was Locke's chief maxim. It is the one most popular today, but it does not seem to me justified by success. For my part I do not see any children more stupid than those who have been much reasoned with. Of all the human faculties, reason which may be said to be compounded of all the rest develops most slowly and with greatest difficulty. Yet it is reason that people want to use in the development of the first faculties. A reasonable man is the masterwork of a good education: and we actually pretend to be educating children by means of reason! That is beginning at the end. If children appreciated reason they would not need to be educated. . . .

Nature wants children to be children before they are men. If we deliberately depart from this order we shall get premature fruits which are neither ripe nor well flavoured and which soon decay. We shall have youthful sages and grown up children. Childhood has ways of seeing, thinking and feeling peculiar to itself: nothing can be more foolish than to seek to substitute our ways for them. I should as soon expect a child of ten to be five feet in height as to be possessed of judgment.

Let us lay down as an incontestable principle that the first impulses of nature are always right. There is no original perversity in the human heart. Of every vice we can say how it entered and whence it came. The only passion natural to man is self-love, or self-esteem in a broad sense. This self-esteem has no necessary reference to other people. In so far as it relates to ourselves it is good and useful. It only becomes good or bad in the social application we make of it. . . .

. . . Here comes Emile, and at his approach I have a thrill of joy in which I see he shares. . . . Health glows in his face. His firm step gives him an air of vigour. . . .

His ideas are limited but precise. If he knows nothing by heart, he knows a great deal by experience. If he is not as good a reader in books as other children, he reads better in the book of nature. His mind is not in his tongue but in his head. He has less memory and more judgment. He only knows one language, but he understands what he says; and if he does not talk as well as other children he can do things better than they can. . . .

Work and play are all the same to him. His games are his occupations: he is not aware of any difference. He goes into everything he does with a pleasing interest and freedom. . . .

Emile has lived a child's life and has arrived at the maturity of childhood, without any sacrifice of happiness in the achievement of his own perfection. He has acquired all the reason possible for his age, and in doing so has been as free and as happy as his nature allowed him to be. . . .

Book III

. . . With the child's advance in intelligence other considerations compel greater care in the choice of his occupations. . . .

When children foresee their needs their intelligence has made real progress. They begin to know the value of time. For this reason, it is important to accustom them to employ their time on objects of an obvious utility that are within their understanding. . . . Our real teachers are experience and feeling, and no one ever appreciates what is proper to manhood till he enters into its situations. . . .

Here is our child, ready to cease being a child and to enter on an individual life. More than ever he feels the necessity which binds him to things. After training his body and his senses, we have trained his mind and his judgment. In short, we have combined the use of his limbs with that of his faculties. We have made him an efficient thinking being and nothing further remains for us in the production of a complete man but to make him a loving, sensitive being: in fact, to perfect reason through sentiment. . . .

To begin with, our pupil had only sensations, now he has ideas: he had only feelings, now he judges . . . .

In sensation, judgment is purely passive--we feel what we feel: in perception or idea, it is active--it connects, compares, determines relations. It is never the sensation that is wrong but the judgment passed on it. . . .

I will be told that in training the child to judge, I am departing from nature. I do not think so. Nature chooses her instruments, and makes use of them not according to opinion but according to necessity. There is a great deal of difference between natural man living in nature and natural man living in the social state. Emile is not a savage to be banished to the deserts: he is a savage made to live in a town. He must know how to get a living in towns, and how to get on with their inhabitants, and to live with them, if not to live like them. . . .

Emile, who has been compelled to learn for himself and use his reason, has a limited knowledge, but the knowledge he has is his own, none of it half-known. . . . He has a universal mind, not because of what he knows but from his faculty for acquiring knowledge: a mind open, intelligent, responsive, and (as Montaigne says) if not instructed, capable of being instructed. I am content if he knows the "wherefore" of all he does, and the "why" of all he believes. . . .

Book IV

. . . But man is not meant to be a child for ever. At the time prescribed by nature he passes out of his childhood. As the fretting of the sea precedes the distant storm, this disturbing change is announced by the murmur of nascent passions. . . .

The passions are the chief instruments for our preservation. The child's first sentiment is self-love, the only passion that is born with man. The second, which is derived from it, is the love he has for the people he sees ready to help him, and from this develops a kindly feeling for mankind. But with fresh needs and growing dependence on others comes the consciousness of social relations and with it the sense of duties and preferences. It is at this point that the child may become domineering, jealous, deceitful, vindictive. Self-love being concerned only with ourselves is content when our real needs are satisfied, but self-esteem which involves comparisons with other people never is and never can be content because it makes the impossible demand that others should prefer us to themselves. That is how it comes that the gentle kindly passions issue from self-love, while hate and anger spring from self-esteem. Great care and skill are required to prevent the human heart being depraved by the new needs of social life.

. . . Self-esteem is a useful instrument but it has its dangers. Often it wounds the hand that employs it and rarely does good without also doing evil. Emile, comparing himself with other human beings and finding himself very fortunately situated, will be tempted to give credit to his own reason for the work of his guardian, and to attribute to his own merit the effects of his good fortune. He will say: "I am wise, and men are foolish." This is the error most to be feared, because it is the one hardest to eradicate. . . .

There is no remedy for vanity but experience. . . . Do not waste your time on fine arguments and try to convince an adolescent that he is a man like other men and subject to the same weaknesses. Make him feel it for himself, or he will never learn it. . . .

When I see young people confined to the speculative studies at the most active time of life and then cast suddenly into the world of affairs without the least experience, I find it as contrary to reason as to nature and am not at all surprised that so few people manage their lives well. By some strange perversity we are taught all sorts of useless things, but nothing is done about the art of conduct. We are supposed to be getting trained for society but are taught as if each one of us were going to live a life of contemplation in a solitary cell. You think you are preparing children for life when you teach them certain bodily contortions and meaningless strings of words. I also have been a teacher of the art of conduct. I have taught my Emile to live his own life, and more than that, to earn his own bread. But that is not enough. To live in a world one must get on with people and know how to get a hold on them. . . .

It is by doing good that we become good. I know of no surer way. Keep your pupil occupied with all the good deeds within his power. Let him help poor people with money and with service, and get justice for the oppressed. Active benevolence will lead him to reconcile the quarrels of his comrades and to be concerned about the sufferings of the afflicted. By putting his kindly feelings into action in this way and drawing his own conclusions from the outcome of his efforts, he will get a great deal of useful knowledge. In addition to college lore he will acquire the still more important ability of applying his knowledge to the purposes of life. . . .

DISCUSSION

Rousseau provides us with much to consider and evaluate. Emile, his imaginary pupil, represents us all, as far as Rousseau is concerned. The prospects he has in mind for Emile, therefore, are applicable to educational reform in general. Rousseau attempts to <u>describe</u> what human nature is like before he <u>prescribes</u> how we should be taught. This is a wise plan of action that was adopted, as we have seen, by Plato as well.

What is human nature like? Rousseau presents an interesting picture with wide ramifications. At bottom, we are all, like Emile, "savages made to live in a town." Guided by our impulses and feelings, we are to develop our self-love which is "the only passion born within man." We must take great care in this development, for there are potential dangers lying before us. Whenever we are in a society and related to others, competition can arise and "hate and anger" can arise. This is not a necessary consequence, but we have to work hard at avoiding it. Out of our natural self-love, we can produce kindness and fellow-feelings for others. Self-love, like all else which comes from nature, is good and worthy of promotion. But natural things can become bad in a society which is not careful to nurture our natural tendencies in the right way. The savage in us is "noble", but it can become evil and dangerous.

Above all, educational reform must recognize the "real teachers" of "experience and feelings." From these we form ideas and judgments. It is here that we must be careful, because no sensation is wrong, "only judgments are wrong." It follows that true ideas and judgments are well grounded in our feelings and experiences. This is Rousseau's version of "to thine own self be true", or of Socrates' "know thyself."

This, then, is Rousseau's message: to be educated we must know our true selves. And we are all indebted to him for pointing out the dangers of a society which can too often hide us from ourselves! But the message does not end here. K n o w i n g ourselves and t h i n k i n g for ourselves is only the beginning. For Rousseau, it is not knowing or thinking but doing which is most important of all. "It is by doing good that we become good" he says. And we must all learn to apply our "knowledge to the purposes of life."

Discussion   Questions

1. Rousseau does criticize Locke's maxim "Reason with Children." But do you see other areas where Rousseau seems to agree with Locke? Explain.

2. Do you think that Rousseau is right about the trustworthyness of the "impulses of nature" and our "feelings." Explain what may be a problem here.

3. Rousseau believed that we spend too much time concerning ourselves with what others think, and not enough time with what we think? Do you agree? Discuss.

4. Discuss what you think Rousseau means by "self-love" and "self-esteem." Are they different? Should both be promoted within education? How could this be done?

5. What elements within contemporary education would Rousseau most criticize? Discuss. Are there any current or traditional trends he would applaud? Explain.

CHAPTER SIX

JOHANN FREDERICH HERBART

Johann Frederich Herbart pioneered the systematic study of educational pedagogy. By concentrating on educational process and method as they relate to the teacher, he laid the foundation for a science of education, which later educators would refine and expand.

Born in Oldenberg, Germany on May 4, 1776, Herbart's intellectual development was directed by his mother, a firm disciplinarian skilled in Greek and mathematics. He entered the Gymnasium of Oldenberg and while still in his teens produced distinguished essays regarding moral freedom. He studied philosophy at the University of Jena but left before graduation to tutor in Switzerland for the family of Herr von Steiger. This was Herbart's only experience teaching children and would serve as the basis for the development and refinement of his educational thought.

While in Switzerland, Herbart visited and became familiar with the ideas of Johann Pestalozzi. While attempting to scientifically formalize Pestalozzi's work, Herbart moved to the University of Gottingen where he created his own pedagogical system. In 1809 he became the chair of philosophy at Konigsberg where he established a pedagogical seminary in conjunction with a practice school. His purpose was to infuse scientific experimentation and research into the development and practice of educational methodology, an approach presently employed for educational study by a majority of universities.

Herbart was the first to create a system of education based on psychology. He rejected the theory of separate mental faculties, insisting that our minds develop from a constant flow of ideas or presentations. These ideas are mental forces working within the mind to preserve their existence. Feelings and emotions grow out of the interaction of ideas in our consciousness. This interaction is the process of apperception, in which new ideas are evaluated and processed by those already present in consciousness. As the mind strives for equilibrium, apperception results in the retention, modification, combination, or elimination of ideas based on their compatibility with existing ideas. This process results in the formation of the apperceptive mass and establishes the foundation for Herbart's theory of education.

To gain the attention and interest of students, teachers must relate new material to the pupils' previous knowledge or experience. Herbart stressed mental expansion through broad-based, interdisciplinary instruction and the creation of the many-sided interest. He believed that students' interest centered around knowledge, consisting of empirical, speculative, and aesthetic ideas, and participation, consisting of sympathetic, social, and religious ideas. Instruction, if many-sidedness is to be achieved, should be based on a correlated curriculum which studies both historical and scientific study. Thus, the entire range of ideas can be addressed in a unified, integrated manner.

To enhance the opportunity for student success, Herbart developed a system of instruction based on students acquiring facts and assimilating them. Students move back and forth in this two-part mental process of absorption and reflection. Based on this process, Herbart developed his four-step outline for method of instruction: (1) clearness: presenting of concepts to be learned; (2) association: organizing and relating new concepts to previous knowledge; (3) system: analyzing and arranging concepts into logical relationships; and (4) method:

applying relationships to new information. Herbart emphasized that teachers should consider these steps if instruction is to be meaningful and expand interest. This resulted in the educational process becoming sequenced and outcome-oriented, guided by the objective method of presentation, and possible application of planned instruction.

Herbart's influence on the application of applied psychology to instruction and his contribution to educational pedagogy cannot be denied. Much of his work lies at the heart of present educational research and practice. Yet an examination of Herbart's educational thought would not be complete without examining what he believed to be the ultimate goal of education, the development of moral character. He maintained that education should create well-rounded, holistic individuals, with varied interests, and solid, socially acceptable moral characters. Misconduct and unacceptable behavior were the result of inadequate education. First, it was the teacher's duty to insure that each student become properly socialized through instruction, the process of presenting material to students in order to expand thinking and develop many-sided interest. Second, discipline would be necessary to keep students attentive so instruction could successfully develop their will. Finally, training would work in conjunction with instruction and discipline to form the will of each child through actual experience. While discipline forces children to act correctly, if education were handled properly and teachers modeled morally correct behavior, children would eventually act correctly according to their own will.

Herbart's emphasis on education's role of moral development, the development of moral character being education's major aim, is clearly expressed in the following reading. This was Herbart's last definitive attempt to systematically describe his educational beliefs. These excerpts from Herbart's *Outlines* speak clearly to what he believed was the purpose of education.

HERBART ON THE EDUCATION OF MORAL CHARACTER*

The Ethical Basis of Instruction

8. The term *virtue* expresses the whole purpose of education. Virtue is the idea of inner freedom which has developed into an abiding actuality in an individual. Whence, as inner freedom is a relation between insight and volition, a double task is at once set before the teacher. It becomes his business to make actual each of these factors separately, in order that later a permanent relationship may result.

9. But even here at the outset we need to bear in mind the identity of morality with the effort put forth to realize the permanent actuality of the harmony between insight and volition. To induce the pupil to make this effort is a difficult achievement; at all events, it becomes possible only when the twofold training mentioned above is well under way. It is easy enough, by a study of the example of others, to cultivate theoretical acumen; the moral application to the pupil himself, however, can be made, with the hope of success, only is so far as his inclinations and habits have taken a direction in keeping with his insight. If such is not the case, there is danger lest the pupil, after all, knowingly subordinate his correct theoretical judgment to mere prudence. It is thus that evil in the strict sense originates.

10. Of the remaining practical or ethical concepts, the idea of perfection points to health of body and mind; it implies a high regard for both, and their systematic cultivation.

---

* **Source**: Johann Frederich Herbart, **Outlines of Educational Doctrine**, trans., Alexis F. Lenge (New York: The Macmillan Company, 1901).

11. The idea of good-will counsels the educator to ward off temptation to ill-will as long as such temptation might prove dangerous. It is essential, on the other hand, to imbue the pupil with a feeling of respect for good-will.

12. The idea of justice demands that the pupil abstain from contention. It demands, furthermore, reflection on strife, so that respect for justice may strike deep root.

13. The idea of equity is especially involved in cases where the pupil has merited punishment as requital for the intentional infliction of pain. Here the degree of punishment must be carefully ascertained and acknowledged as just.

14. Where a number of pupils are assembled there arises, naturally, on a small scale, a system of laws and rewards. This system, and the demands which in the world at large spring from the same ideas, must be brought into accord.

15. The concept of an administrative system has great significance for pedagogics, since every pupil, whatever his rank or social status, must be trained for cooperation in the social whole to fit him for usefulness. This requirement may assume very many different forms.

16. Of the system of civilization only the aspect of general culture, not that of special training, must be emphasized at this point.

17. For the business of education, the idea of perfection, while it does not rise into excessive prominence, stands out above all others on account of its uninterrupted application. The teacher discovers in the as yet undeveloped human being a force which requires his incessant attention to intensify, to direct, and to concentrate.

18. The constant presence of the idea of perfection easily introduces a false feature into moral education in the strict sense. The pupil may get an erroneous impression as to the relative importance of the lessons, practice, and performance demanded of him, and so be betrayed into the belief that he is essentially perfect when these demands are satisfied.

19. For this reason alone, if others were wanting, it is necessary to combine moral education proper, which in everyday life lays stress continually on correct self-determination, with religious training. The notion that something really worthy has been achieved needs to be tempered by humility. Conversely, religious education has need of the moral also to forestall cant and hypocrisy, which are only too apt to appear where morality has not already secured a firm foothold through earnest self-questioning and self-criticism with a view to improvement. Finally, inasmuch as moral training must be put off until after insight and right habits have been acquired, religious education, too, should not be begun too early; nor should it be needlessly delayed.

The Aim of Instruction

62. The ultimate purpose of instruction is contained in the notion, virtue. But in order to realize the final aim, another and nearer one must be set up. We may term it, *many-sidedness of interest*. The word *interest* stands in general for that kind of mental activity which it is the business of instruction to incite. Mere information does not suffice; for this we think of as a supply or store of facts, which a person might possess or lack, and still remain the same being. But he who lays hold of his information and reaches out for more, takes an interest in it. Since, however, this mental activity is varied (60), we need to add the further determination supplied by the term *many-sidedness*.

63. We may speak also of indirect as distinguished from direct interest. But a predominance of indirect interest tends to one-

sidedness, if not to selfishness. The interest of the selfish man in anything extends only so far as he can see advantages or disadvantages to himself. In this respect the one-sided man approximates the selfish man, although the fact may escape his own observation; since he relates everything to the narrow sphere for which he lives and thinks. Here lies his intellectual power, and whatever does not interest him as means to his limited ends, becomes an impediment.

64. As regards the bearings of interest on virtue, we need to remember that many-sidedness of interest alone, even of direct interest such as instruction is to engender, is yet far from being identical with virtue itself; also that, conversely, the weaker the original mental activity, the less likelihood that virtue will be realized at all, not to speak of the variety of manifestation possible in action. Imbeciles cannot be virtuous. Virtue involves an awakening of mind.

65. Scattering no less than one-sidedness forms an antithesis to many-sidedness. Many-sidedness is to be the basis of virtue; but the latter is an attribute of personality, hence it is evident that the unity of self-consciousness must be impaired. The business of instruction is to form the person on many sides, and accordingly to avoid a distracting or dissipating effect. And instruction has successfully avoided this in the case of one who with ease surveys his well-arranged knowledge *in all of its unifying relations* and holds it together as *his very own.*

DISCUSSION

Herbart insists that if moral character or virtue is to exist, education must develop the inner freedom. Evil does not occur naturally but rises from a lack of effective education. Through instruction, discipline, and training the individual must attain insight into socially acceptable behavior and become inclined to act in accordance with those insights. Thus, moral understanding and conduct must coincide in the virtuous individual.

The concepts of perfection, good will, justice and equity must also be a part of moral development. Perfection refers to an efficient will, in which the individual has direction, vigor, and harmony of purpose. Behavior is positively oriented, with vacillation and indecision eliminated. Good will or benevolence is the concern for the welfare of others. Justice refers to the concept of rights, in which all individuals' behavior must conform to the existing social structures. Equity provides the foundation for society's system of rewards and punishments.

Herbart firmly believed that the concepts of moral education should be combined with religious training. This combination would serve as a balance, providing humility to the practice of self-determination. The result would be a morally religious individual.

If this result is to be accomplished, if education is to arrive at its ultimate aim, the erection of many-sidedness of interest must be achieved. Knowledge must be exposed to students as an integrated whole, by which students can arrange it in a unified fashion and strive for more. Virtue is attained by the stimulation of mental activity, which creates a person of many dimensions.

Discussion Questions

1. Why did Herbart's beliefs regarding psychology lead to his creation of a systematic educational pedagogy?

2. How do presentations lead to an apperceptive mass?

3. How does Herbart's four-step instruction system relate to recent lesson preparation?

4. Why would Herbart oppose extremely restrictive classroom discipline?

5. What would you emphasize as key components of moral character? How would you convey them to students?

CHAPTER SEVEN

HORACE MANN

If, as the Greek tragedian Aeschylus claims that "...wisdom comes alone through suffering," then Horace Mann was truly prepared to champion the cause of public education. Despite a bleak and difficult childhood, Mann became a leader, educator, and spokesman for children and their education throughout his state of Massachusetts and the world. Indeed, his hard work and boundless energy in the cause of universal education won him the worthy title of Father of the American Public School.

Born May 4, 1796, Mann was the fourth child of a Franklin, Massachusetts farming family with strict Puritan morals. He led a simple life, filled with hard work and little opportunity for education. Although his parents were enthusiastic about the importance of learning, schooling was only available several weeks in the winter. The schools were desolate structures, with poor ventilation and lighting, uncomfortable furnishings, and little educational equipment. Teachers were often ill-prepared for their assignments and discipline was severe. At the age of thirteen Mann's father, Thomas, died and life became a struggle of poverty and hardship. Mann suffered health problems that persisted throughout his life.

Through the encouragement of an itinerant schoolmaster named Mr. Barrett, Mann, at age fifteen, began to study Latin and Greek in order to gain admittance to college. Within six months he was admitted to the sophomore class of Brown University, where he graduated in 1819 as the valedictorian. Mann tutored briefly before entering Judge Tapping Reeve's law school in Litchfield, Connecticut. Upon admittance to the bar, he moved to Boston to establish a law practice. He became an extremely successful jurist, amassing a sizable estate and the respect of the Boston elite. He married Charlotte Messer, daughter of the Brown University president, whom he met while living at the Messer home as a student.

Mann served in the Massachusetts state legislature where he supported humanitarian causes of longtime friends Dr. Samuel G. Howe, pioneer of education for the blind, and Dorothea Dix, leader in the humane treatment of the mentally retarded. His political future appeared bright until the tragic, unexpected death of his wife left him brooding, melancholy and detached from the interests that once fired his energies and imagination. However, an opportunity was to arise that would provide the catalyst for Mann's educational achievements and professional legacy.

In 1837, the Massachusetts legislature created the State Board of Education, the first of its kind in the United States. Although common schools had existed in Massachusetts for nearly two centuries, the State Board of Education was given the responsibility to revise and reorganize them. The Board requested that Horace Mann become their first Secretary, making him the equivalent of a state superintendent of schools. Few friends or colleagues encouraged him to accept this low paying position, which was advisory in nature and provided no enforcement powers. Mann, however, saw the duties of Secretary as an opportunity to serve and elevate mankind, through the improvement of education. He quickly gave up his lucrative law practice and promising political career, and immersed himself in his new responsibilities.

Given the task of organizing Massachusetts' district and township schools into a single state system placed Mann at the heart of an emotional, political structure which would change the very fabric of public education. Impeding his progress were selfish interests of narrow-minded legislators, intransigent teachers, sectarian preachers, skeptical businessmen, and taxpayers suffering the strains of the country's worst financial depression. Since Massachusetts was convinced their schools were the nation's best, he had to contend with the public's inertia regarding educational reform. With no authority to command change, Mann was left to his powers of persuasion to pursue school improvement. Mann believed, however, that enlightenment, not coercion, was the ideal method of informing the citizenry of what was at stake and marshaling their support. Mann read extensively, collected statistics and information regarding school conditions, attended and spoke at county conferences, and visited schools throughout the state to dialogue with local officials and interested members of the public. He formulated the principles that would shape and define his educational philosophy, while garnering the intellectual and financial backing of the Massachusetts' citizens.

Mann rejected the evils of an Old World class system that provided education and refinement to one group, relegating the remainder to menial labor and illiteracy. In a nation with a recently formed democratic government, an informed, literate electorate was a necessity that would insure stability and growth. Public schools would provide a national identity and unity of purpose in which people would have the capacity for governing themselves through critical examination of the issues and enlightened suffrage. Civic responsibility would be achieved through non-sectarian, moral schools that would stress practical morality and democratic ideals, not based on a single creed or doctrine but representative of a collective common culture. Emphasis would be placed on the development of intelligence, as well as on the highest morals and values of the common culture.

Mann was convinced that every person had an absolute right to education. Universal education would preserve and fortify human dignity, while developing every child's individual, intrinsic capacities for limitless improvement and progress. Schools would be free, receiving their financial support from state and local governments. This system would provide equal opportunity to all citizens by providing an equivalent quality of education to that of expensive private schools. To maintain interest and support which would be vital for continued success, the public, through the legislature and local schools boards, would administer and regulate their own public schools.

Mann's view of universal public education had its detractors that were predisposed to an opposing viewpoint. However, the logical principles with which Mann supported his conception of education slowly eroded their antagonism and garnered their praise. Wealthy people and businessmen responded to Mann's stewardship theory. This theory helped them to recognize their responsibility for providing equality of educational opportunity, which in turn would produce an intelligent, conscientious, and innovative work force that would serve to strengthen and bolster their businesses and communities. Lower class people, workers and farmers were drawn to the proposition that public education would be the great equalizer, providing their children with the necessary skills to improve their status, while producing greater economic opportunity and mobility.

To improve the quality and appeal of his public education movement, Mann worked diligently to improve the caliber and value of its most visible asset, the teacher. Mann recognized the need for instructors with sound educational backgrounds, trained in the philosophy, psychology, and pedagogy of classroom teaching. To achieve this, Mann was instrumental in the establishment of normal schools, two-year institutions designed to improve teaching. By striving for better preparation, higher salaries, and public recognition, Mann raised teaching to professional stature.

Mann developed two sources to disseminate information, maintain reform momentum, and cultivate public support. He founded and edited the *Common School Journal* as a means of promoting public awareness of educational issues. However, his most powerful instrument of educational reform were his twelve "Annual Reports" to the State Board of Education. Through these documents, Mann described the conditions within the schools, progress that had been made, necessary changes that should be pursued, and the educational philosophy behind the entire public education movement. Through his writings he attempted to direct political, as well as public opinion. His reports provided a detailed account of public school growth under Mann's leadership.

The Seventh Report, 1843, is probably the most significant, marking the pivotal turning point between Mann and his detractors. The reform movement had been progressing steadily through Mann's early years as Secretary. The public and the legislature had been responsive to the changes in the common school system, as adversaries searched for a means to stop the momentum. Mann traveled to Europe with his second wife Mary Peabody Mann to visit their education facilities and speak with teachers. Mann witnessed an abundance of teaching methods and techniques which he believed would improve education in America. He was uniquely impressed with German schools' use of oral instruction, teacher-student mutual acceptance, manipulatives, and the disdain for corporal punishment.

Upon his return, he included his observations and opinions of European education in his Seventh Report, and suggested that Massachusetts schools could benefit through the implementation of these approaches. This raised the ire of the Boston schoolmasters and motivated them to respond with a stinging attack on Mann and his ideas. This grew into the last major confrontation between Mann and opponents of his public school movement. Charges and counter charges were made, but in the end the detractors could not stop the progressive movement which Mann had created. Influential friends came to his aid with five thousand dollars which was matched by the State Legislature and earmarked for school improvement. Public education was clearly viewed as a service to the welfare of mankind. Progress would not be hindered or stopped.

Mann resigned as Secretary in 1848 to represent Massachusetts in the United States House of Representatives, taking the seat of John Quincy Adams who had recently died. Mann, like Adams, was an opponent of slavery and he became a spokesman for abolition in Washington. He moved on from political life once again to pursue an opportunity of educational leadership. He spent his remaining years as President of Antioch College in Ohio. His ideal of equal opportunity was reflected in Antioch College's practice of accepting students of both sexes and all races.

To summarize Mann's contribution to society, these words from his last speech to the 1859 graduating class serve to personify his ideals and his life. "...BE ASHAMED TO DIE UNTIL YOU HAVE WON SOME VICTORY FOR HUMANITY." Truly, Horace Mann has no reason for shame.

Mann delivered the following address at county conventions throughout Massachusetts to bolster support for the goals and reforms of the newly formed State Board of Education. In this passage titled "The Purpose of Education," Mann delineates the principles and values that he believes should be the foundation of public education.

MANN'S PURPOSES OF EDUCATION*

Such are some of the most obvious topics, belonging to that sacred work, -- the education of children. The science, or philosophical principles on which this work is to be conducted; the art, or manner in which those principles are to be applied, must all be rightly settled and generally understood, before any system of Public Instruction can operate with efficiency. Yet all this has been mainly left to chance. Compared with its deserts, how disproportionate, how little, the labor, cost and talent, devoted to it. We have a Congress, convening annually, at almost incredible expense, to decide upon questions of tariff, internal improvement, and currency. We have a State Legislature, continuing in session more than a fourth part of every year, to regulate our internal polity. We have Courts, making continual circuits through the Commonwealth, to adjudicate upon doubtful rights of person or property, however trivial. Every great department of literature and of business has its Periodical. Every part, political, religious, and social, has its Press. Yet Education, that vast cause, of which all other causes are only constituent parts; that cause, on which all other causes are dependent, for their vitality and usefulness, -- if I except the American Institute of Instruction, and a few local, feeble, unpatronized, though worthy associations, -- Education has literally nothing, in the way of comprehensive organization and of united effort, acting for a common end and under the focal light of a common intelligence. It is under these circumstances; it is in view of these great public wants, that the Board of Education has been established, -- not to legislate, not to enforce, -- but to collect facts, to educe principles, to diffuse a knowledge of improvements; -- in fine, to submit the views

---

* Source: Horace Mann, **Lecture on Education** (Boston: Mersh, Capen, Lyon and Webb, 1840).

of men who have thought much upon this subject to men who have thought but little.

To specify the labors, which education has yet to perform, would be only to pass in review the varied interests of humanity. Its general purposes are to preserve the good and to repudiate the evil which now exists, and to give scope to the sublime law of progression. It is its duty to take the accumulations in knowledge of almost six thousand years, and to transfer the vast treasure to posterity. Suspend its functions for but one generation, and the experience and achievements of the past are lost. The race must commence its fortunes, anew, and must again spend six thousand years, before it can grope its way upward from barbarism to the present point of civilization. With the wisdom, education must also teach something of the follies, of the past, for admonition and warning; for it has been well said, that mankind have seldom arrived at truth, on any subject, until they had first exhausted its errors.

Education is to instruct the whole people in the proper care of the body, in order to augment the powers of that wonderful machine, and to prevent so much of disease, of suffering, and of premature death. The body is the mind's instrument; and the powers of the mind, like the skill of an artisan, may all be baffled, through the imperfection of their utensils. The happiness and the usefulness of thousands and tens of thousands of men and women have been destroyed, from not knowing a few of the simple laws of health, which they might have learned in a month; -- nay, which might have been so impressed upon them, in childhood, as habits, that they would never think there was any other way. I do not speak of the ruin, that comes from slavery to throned appetites, where the bondage might continue in defiance of knowledge; but I speak of cases, where the prostration of noble powers and the suffering of terrible maladies result from sheer ignorance and false views of the wise laws to which God has subjected our physical nature. No doubt, Voltaire said truly, that the fate of many a nation had depended upon the good or bad digestion of its minister; and how much more extensively true would the remark be, if applied to individuals? How many men perfectly understand the observances by which their horses and cattle are made healthy and strong; while their children are puny, distempered, and have chronic diseases, at the very earliest age, at which so highly-finished an article as a chronic disease can be prepared. There is a higher art than the art of the physician; -- the art, not of *restoring*, but of *making* health. Health is a product. Health is a manufactured article, -- as much so as any fabric of the loom or the workshop; and, except in some few cases of hereditary taint or of organic lesion from accident or violence, the how much, or the how little, health any man shall enjoy, depends upon his treatment of himself; or rather, upon the treatment of those who manage his infancy and childhood, and create his habits for him. Situated, as we are, in a high latitude, with the Atlantic ocean on one side and a range of mountains on the other, we cannot escape frequent and great transitions, in the temperature of our weather. Our region is the perpetual battleground of the torrid and the arctic, where they alternately prevail; and it is only by a sort of average that we call it *temperate.* Yet to this natural position we must adapt ourselves, or abandon it, or suffer. Hence the necessity of making health, in order to endure natural inclemencies; and hence the necessity of including the simple and benign laws on which it depends, in all our plans of education. Certainly, our hearts should glow with gratitude to Heaven, for all the means of health; but every expression indicating that health is a Divine gift, in any other sense than all our blessings are a Divine gift, should be discarded from the language; and it should be incorporated into the forms of speech, that a man prepares his own health, as he does his own house.

Education is to inspire the love of truth, as the supremest good, and to clarify the vision of the intellect to discern it. We want a generation of men above deciding great and eternal principles, upon narrow and selfish grounds. Our advanced state of civilization has evolved many complicated questions respecting social duties. We want a generation of men capable of taking up these complex questions, and of turning all sides of them towards the sun, and of examining them by the white light of reason, and not under the false colors which sophistry may throw upon them. We want no men who will change, like the vanes of our steeples, with the course of the popular wind; but we want men who, like mountains, will change the course of the wind. We want no more of those patriots who exhaust their patriotism, in lauding the past; but we want patriots who will do for the future what the past has done for us. We want men capable of deciding, not merely what is right, in principle, -- *that* is often the smallest part of the case; but we want men capable of deciding what is right in means, to accomplish what is right in principle. We want men who will speak to this great people in counsel, and not in flattery. We want godlike men who can tame the madness of the times and, speaking divine words in a divine spirit, can say to the raging of human passions, "Peace, be still;" and usher in the calm of enlightened reason and conscience. Look at our community, divided into so many parties and factions, and these again subdivided, on all questions of social, national, and international, duty; -- while, over all stands, almost unheeded, the sublime form of Truth, eternally and indissolubly *One!* Nay, further, those do not agree in thought who agree in words. Their unanimity is a delusion. It arises from the imperfection of language. Could men, who subscribe to the same forms of words, but look into each other's minds, and see, there, what features their own idolized doctrines wear, friends would often start back from the friends they have loved, with as much abhorrence as from the enemies they have persecuted. Now, what can save us from endless contention, but the love of truth? What can save us, and our children after us, from eternal, implacable, universal war, but the greatest of all human powers, -- the power of impartial thought? Many, -- may I not say most, -- of those great questions, which make the present age boil and seethe, like a cauldron, will never be settled, until we have a generation of men who were educated, from childhood, to seek for truth and to revere justice. In the middle of the last century, a great dispute arose among astronomers, respecting one of the planets. Some, in their folly, commenced a war of words, and wrote hot books against each other; others, in their wisdom, improved their telescopes, and soon settled the question forever. Education should imitate the latter. If there are momentous questions which, with present lights, we cannot demonstrate and determine, let us rear up stronger, and purer, and more impartial, minds, for the solemn arbitrament. Let it be for ever and ever inculcated, that no bodily wounds or maim; no deformity of person, nor disease of brain, or lungs, or heart, can be so disabling or so painful as error; and that he who heals us of our prejudices is a thousand-fold more our benefactor, than he who heals us of mortal maladies. Teach children, if you will, to beware of the bite of a mad dog; but teach them still more faithfully, that no horror of water is so fatal as a horror of truth, because it does not come from our leader or our party. Then shall we have more men who will think, as it were, under oath; -- not thousandth and ten thousandth transmitters of falsity; -- not copyists of copyists, and blind followers of blind followers; but men who can track the Deity in his ways of wisdom. A love of truth, -- *a love of truth*; this is the pool of a moral Bethesda, whose waters have miraculous healing. And though we lament that we cannot bequeath to posterity this precious boon, in its perfectness, as the greatest of all patrimonies, yet let us rejoice that we can inspire a love of it, a reverence for it, a devotion to it; and thus circumscribe and weaken whatever is wrong, and enlarge and strengthen whatever is right, in the mixed inheritance of good and evil, which, in the order of Providence, one generation transmits to another.

If we contemplate the subject with the eye of a statesman, what resources are there, in the whole domain of Nature, at all comparable to that vast influx of power which comes into the world with every incoming generation of children? Each embryo life is more wonderful than the globe it is sent to inhabit, and more glorious than the sun upon which it first opens its eyes. Each one of these millions, with a fitting education, is capable of adding something to the sum of human happiness, and of subtracting something from the sum of human misery; and many great souls amongst them there are, who may become instruments for turning the course of nations, as the rivers of water are turned. It is the duty of moral and religious education to employ and administer all these capacities of good, for lofty purposes of human beneficence, -- as a wise minister employs the resources of a great empire. "Suffer little children to come unto me," said the Savior, "and forbid them not, for of such is the kingdom of Heaven." And who shall dare say, that philanthropy and religion cannot make a better world than the present, from beings like those in the kingdom of Heaven!

Education must be universal. It is well, when the wise and the learned discover new truths; but how much better to diffuse the truths already discovered, amongst the multitude! Every addition to true knowledge is an addition to human power; and while a philosopher is discovering one new truth, millions may be propagated amongst the people. Diffusion, then, rather than discovery, is the duty of our government. With us, the qualification of voters is as important as the qualification of governors, and even comes first, in the natural order. Yet there is no Sabbath of rest, in our contests about the latter, while so little is done to qualify the former. The theory of our government is, -- not that all men, however unfit, shall be voters, -- but that every man, by the power of reason and the sense of duty, shall become fit to be a voter. Education must bring the practice as nearly as possible to the theory. As the children now are, so will the sovereigns soon be. How can we expect the fabric of the government to stand, if vicious materials are daily wrought into its frame-work? Education must prepare our citizens to become municipal officers, intelligent jurors, honest witnesses, legislators, or competent judges of legislation, -- in fine, to fill all the manifold relations of life. For this end, it must be universal. The whole land must be watered with the streams of knowledge. It is not enough to have, here and there, a beautiful fountain playing in palace gardens; but let it come like the abundant fatness of the clouds upon the thirsting earth.

Finally, education, alone, can conduct us to that enjoyment which is, at once, best in quality and infinite in quantity. God has revealed to us, -- not by ambiguous signs, but by his mighty works; -- not in disputable language of human invention; -- but by the solid substance and reality of things, what He holds to be valuable, and what He regards as of little account. The latter He has created sparingly, as though it were nothing worth; while the former He has poured forth with immeasurable munificence. I suppose all the diamonds ever found, could be hid under a bushel. The quantity is little, because the value is small. But iron-ore, -- without which man-kind would always have been barbarians; without which they would now relapse into barbarism, -- He has strewed profusely all over the earth. Compare the scantiness of pearl with the extent of forests and coal-fields. Of one, little has been created, because it is worth little; of the others, much, because they are worth much. His fountains of naphtha, how few, and myrrh and frankincense, how exiguous; but who can fathom his reservoirs of water, or measure the light and the air! This principle pervades every realm of Nature. Creation seems to have been projected upon the plan of increasing the quantity, in the ratio of the intrinsic value. Emphatically is this plan manifested, when we come to that part of creation, we call *ourselves*. Enough of the materials of worldly good have been created to answer this great principle, -- that, up to the point of competence, up to the point of independence and self-respect, few things are more valuable than property; beyond that point, few things are of less. And hence it is, that all acquisitions of property, -- confer an inferior sort of pleasure, in inferior quantities. However rich a man may be, a certain number of thicknesses of woolens or of silks is all he can comfortably wear. Give him a dozen palaces, he can live in but one, at a time. Though the commander be worth the whole regiment, or ship's company, he can have the animal pleasure of eating only his own rations; and any other animal eats, with as much relish as he. Hence the wealthiest, with all their wealth, are driven back to a cultivated mind, to beneficent uses and appropriations; and it is then, and then only, that a glorious vista of happiness opens out into immensity and immortality.

Education, then, is to show to our youth, in early life, this broad line of demarcation between the value of those things which can be owned and enjoyed by but one, and those which can be owned and enjoyed by all. If I own a ship, a house, a farm, or a mass of the metals called precious, my right to them is, in its nature, sole and exclusive. No other man has a right to trade with my ship, to occupy my house, to gather my harvests, or to appropriate my treasures to his use. They are mine, and are incapable, both of a sole and of a joint possession. But not so of the treasures of knowledge, which it is the duty of education to diffuse. The same truth may enrich and ennoble all intelligences at once. Infinite diffusion subtracts nothing from depth. None are made poor because others are made rich. In this part of the Divine economy, the privilege of primogeniture attaches to all; and every son and daughter of Adam is heir to an infinite patrimony. If I own an exquisite picture or statue, it is mine, exclusively. Even though publicly exhibited, but few could be charmed by its beauties, at the same time. It is incapable of bestowing a pleasure, simultaneous and universal. But not so of the beauty of a moral sentiment; not so of the glow of sublime emotions; not so of the feelings of conscious purity and rectitude. These may shed rapture upon all, without deprivation of any; be imparted, and still possessed; transferred to millions, yet never surrendered; carried out of the world, and still left in it. These may imparadise mankind, and undiluted, unattenuated, be sent round the whole orb of being. Let education, then, teach children this great truth, written, as it is, on the fore-front of the universe, that God has so constituted this world, into which He has sent them, that *whatever is really and truly valuable may be possessed by all, and possessed in exhaustless abundance.*

And now, you, my friends! who feel that you are patriots and lovers of mankind, -- what bulwarks, what ramparts for freedom, can you devise, so enduring and impregnable, as intelligence and virtue! Parents! among the happy groups of children whom you have at home, -- more dear to you than the blood in the fountain of life, -- you have not a son nor a daughter who, in this world of temptation, is not destined to encounter perils more dangerous than to walk a bridge of a single plank, over a dark and sweeping torrent, beneath. But is in your power and at your option, with the means which Providence will graciously vouchsafe, to give them that firmness of intellectual movement and that keenness of moral vision, -- that light of knowledge and that omnipotence of virtue, -- by which, in the hour of trial, they will be able to walk, with unfaltering step, over the deep and yawning abyss, below, and to reach the opposite shore, in safety, and honor, and happiness.

DISCUSSION

Mann recognized that if progress toward educational reform was to become a reality, that organization of purpose was necessary. The schools which he was called on to improve had no unified leadership or governing structure. They were separate institutions approaching education from their own particular viewpoint. Mann envisioned a public school system that would require disparate groups to work in concert toward unified goals and objectives. Only through cooperation and consensus could communities provide equal educational opportunity for all its citizens.

Mann believed that education was a force for the advancement of civilization. Schools should convey the wisdom and virtue of preceding generations, while also pointing to their failures and pitfalls, in order that mankind could continue to progress. Failure to maintain this progression toward excellence would result in the decline of civilization and mankind.

The need for physical education in the schools was a priority for Mann, growing out of habitual health problems that persisted from his childhood. The laws of health and hygiene should be stressed so as to become habitual practice among the people, and thus develop a more vibrant, well-conditioned community, free of disease and physical suffering. With healthy bodies, intellectual development is given greater capacity for success.

Mann saw the necessity of the search for truth, and stressed the vital mission of the schools to develop within students the reflection, inquiry, and critical thinking skills necessary for enlightened reasoning. Students must cultivate the skill of impartial thought as a means of discovering truth if successive generations are to cope with the critical issues facing mankind. This thirst for truth stimulates intellectual growth and the development of justice, moral values, civic responsibility, and human compassion.

Finally, Mann trumpeted universal education as the means of diffusing knowledge to the masses. He contended that education was a commodity of inestimable worth and that its value could not be diminished, only enhanced, by making it available to every individual. Equality of educational opportunity serves to elevate the dignity of mankind through the expansion and improvement of the collective human spirit.

Discussion Questions

1. How did Horace Mann's childhood and educational background influence his work as Secretary of the Massachusetts State Board of Education?

2. How did Mann prepare for his work as Secretary? How did he achieve an understanding of the educational situation as it existed in common schools?

3. Why did Mann stress the need for non-sectarian, universal, public education? Did Mann believe that moral or religious teaching have a place in public schools?

4. What impact did Mann's Seventh Annual Report have on the public education reform movement?

5. How did Mann elevate and improve the stature of the teaching profession?

CHAPTER EIGHT

WILLIAM JAMES

Our first psychological theory on education comes from a gentleman who never had a course in psychology in his life. In fact, the first lecture in psychology that James had ever heard was the one he himself delivered to his students at Harvard University. Regarded during his time as the pope of American Psychology, William James was a fascinating combination of American pragmatism and European culture. We will first examine some of the facets of his life, and then turn to a discussion concerning his ideas on education.

William James was born on January 11, 1842 in New York City. This family enjoyed considerable wealth, and he and his siblings knew most of the finer things in life. Their father, Henry James Sr., strongly influenced their early education by expanding their formal schooling in both the United States and Europe. The James' children would spend several years of their life with the finest tutors in England, France, and Italy, and received first hand knowledge of the arts and sciences by visits to the museums and galleries of their day. James was able to speak fluent German, Italian and French, and was comfortable with scholars both home and abroad.

At first James was drawn to the field of art as a career, but shortly after beginning his training he abandoned that choice for the natural sciences. Being quite interested in the questions of philosophy, James undertook a premedical program of study at Harvard, hoping to discover the connections between mind and body. He was later to assert that consciousness cannot be reduced to physiological functioning, a position he held all his life.

At the age of 23 James accepted a position as a research assistant to Louis Agassiz on an expedition into the Amazon Jungle.   The trip was disastrous; he was seasick, homesick, annoyed by the heat and insects, and bored with his job of classification.   He returned to finish his Medical Degree at Harvard in 1869, but knew that because of his bad back and poor vision he would never be a practicing physician.   Still fascinated with the questions of philosophy, but trained as a scientist, James would turn to the study and teaching of psychology as a career.   In 1872 he was offered a faculty position at Harvard, and in the Fall of 1874 he delivered his first lecture in psychology, discussing the relationships between physiology and psychology.

James was a popular instructor, especially noted for his charm, wit and use of metaphor to illustrate his points.   He did, however, find that he could not adequately meet the needs of his wife and five children on a professors salary, so he took to writing and giving outside lectures as a means of supplementing his income.   In 1878 he signed a contract with the Holt Publishing Company to write a major introductory text in Psychology; twelve years later his *Principles of Psychology* was published and was met with widespread success.   The two volume, 1400 page book was followed two years later by an abridged version affectionately known as the "Jimmy" (as opposed to the "James").   His books were translated and used in universities across Europe, as well as in most colleges and universities in the States.   He was without doubt the leading American Psychologist of his day.

Some other aspects of James' life are worth noting.   To begin with, he was not fond of laboratory and mathematical research methods as applied to the science of psychology.   In a famous quote, he stated that "Brass instrument and algebraic formula psychology fills me with horror."   He was however interested in several topics that today are listed under the heading of "parapsychology."   These included telepathy, clairvoyance, fortune telling and other such related areas of psychical investigation.

During the last twenty years of his life James turned more earnestly to matters concerning philosophy. His major contribution to this field were his thoughts on Pragmatism, which is the most original philosophical position in America (some other famous pragmatists are Charles S. Pierce and John Dewey). The pragmatists detest ideas which do not make a difference in real, daily living. "Pragmatism" derives from the common sense or pragmatic--i.e., practical. This view holds that beliefs are real because they work for an individual. This implies a highly phenomenological and subjectively oriented system, as opposed to an all encompassing absolutism. The validity of a belief is ascertained by its practical consequences. For example, if an individual believes that a drug will cure him of an affliction, and in fact the drug does so, then that is the truth of that individual. This is not to say that the belief of one should be imposed on or necessarily accepted by others; beliefs are personal and subjective. Pragmatists were open to both the empirical method as well as morality and religion. Some have suggested that they offered a middle ground between the scientific and the values oriented ideas of religion.

It is clear from James' own writings that he was more dedicated to philosophy than psychology, and expressed a desire to be remembered as a philosopher. Although James did not found a school of psychology nor produce any outstanding research within psychology, he is nevertheless remembered as the champion of American Psychology in 19th century America. His fame is primarily due to his *Principles*, and to his lively and enthusiastic style of lecturing. William James died on August 26, 1910 of a weak heart.

The selected reading from William James is from the 1899 book *Talks to Teachers On Psychology*; and to "Students on Some of Life's Ideals." This book contains advice to teachers on the importance of motivation, attention, memory and other psychological topics. The following selection discusses the concept of habit, and its necessity in instilling the proper behaviors for a successful educational experience.

JAMES ON THE LAWS OF HABIT*

It is very important that teachers should realize the importance of habit, and psychology helps us greatly at this point. We speak, it is true, of good habits and of bad habits; but, when people use the word 'habit,' in the majority of instances it is a bad habit which they have in mind. They talk of the smoking-habit and the swearing-habit and the drinking-habit, but not of the abstention-habit or the moderation-habit or the courage-habit. But the fact is that our virtues are habits as much as our vices. All our life, so far as it has definite form, is but a mass of habits,--pratical, emotional, and intellectual,-- systematically organized for our weal or woe, and bearing us irresistibly toward our destiny, whatever the latter may be.

Since pupils can understand this at a comparatively early age, and since to understand it contributes in no small measure to their feeling of responsibility, it would be well if the teacher were able himself to talk to them of the philosophy of habit in some such abstract terms as I am now about to talk of it to you.

I believe that we are subject to the law of habit in consequence of the fact that we have bodies. The plasticity of the living matter of our nervous system, in short, is the reason why we do a thing with difficulty the first time, but soon do it more and more easily, and finally, with sufficient practice, do it semi-mechanically, or with hardly any consciousness at all. Our nervous systems have (in Dr. Carpenter's words) grown to the way in which they have been exercised, just as a sheet of paper or a coat, once creased or folded, tends to fall forever afterward into the same identical folds.

---

*Source: William James, "The Laws of Habit" from his *Talks to Teachers* given at Cambridge University, Massachusetts in 1892, published in 1899.

Habit is thus a second nature, or rather, as the Duke of Wellington said, it is 'ten times nature,'--at any rate as regards its importance in adult life; for the acquired habits of our training have by that time inhibited or strangled most of the natural implusive tendencies which were originally there. Ninety-nine hundredths or, possibly, nine hundred and ninety-nine thousandths of our activity is purely automatic and habitual, from our rising in the morning to our lying down each night. Our dressing and undressing, our eating and drinking, our greetings and partings, our hat-raisings and giving way for ladies to precede, nay, even most of the forms of our common speech, are things of a type so fixed by repetition as almost to be classed as reflex actions. To each sort of impression we have an automatic, ready-made response. My very words to you now are an example of what I mean; for having already lectured upon habit and printed a chapter about it in a book, and read the latter when in print, I find my tongue inevitably falling into its old phrases and repeating almost literally what I said before.

So far as we are thus mere bundles of habit, we are stereotyped creatures, imitators and copiers of our past selves. And since this, under any circumstances, is what we always tend to become, it follows first of all that the teacher's prime concern should be to ingrain into the pupil that assortment of habits that shall be most useful to him throughout life. Education is for behavior, and habits are the stuff of which behavior consists.

To quote my earlier book directly, the great thing in all education is to make our nervous system our ally instead of our enemy. It is to fund and capitalize our acquisitions, and live at ease upon the interest of the fund. For this we must make automatic and habitual, as early as possible, as many useful actions as we can, and as carefully guard against the growing into ways that are likely to be disadvantageous. The more of the details of our daily life we can hand over to the effortless custody of automatism, the more our higher powers of mind will be set free for their own proper work. There is no more miserable human being than one in whom nothing is habitual but indecision, and for whom the lighting of every cigar, the drinking of every cup, the time of rising and going to bed every day, and the beginning of every bit of work are subjects of express volitional deliberation. Fully half the time of such a man goes to the deciding or regretting of matters which ought to be so ingrained in him as practically not to exist for his consciousness at all. If there be such daily duties not yet ingrained in any one of my hearers, let him begin this very hour to set the matter right.

In Professor Bain's chapter on 'The Moral Habits' there are some admirable practical remarks laid down. Two great maxims emerge from the treatment. The first is that in the acquisition of a new habit, or the leaving off of an old one, we must take care to launch ourselves with as strong and decided an initiative as possible. Accumulate all the possible circumstances which shall reinforce the right motives; put yourself assiduously in conditions that encourage the new way; make engagements incompatible with the old; take a public pledge, if the case allows; in short, envelop your resolution with every aid you know. This will give your new beginning such a momentum that the temptation to break down will not occur as soon as it otherwise might; and every day during which a breakdown is postponed adds to the chances of its not occurring at all....

...The second maxim is, Never suffer an exception to occur till the new habit is securely rooted in your life. Each lapse is like the letting fall of a ball of string which one is carefully winding up: a single slip undoes more than a great many turns will wind again. Continuity of training is the great means of making the nervous system act infallibly right....

...A third maxim may be added to the preceeding pair: Seize the very first possible opportunity to act on every resolution you make, and every emotional prompting you may experience in the direction of the habits you aspire to gain.   It is not in the moment of their forming, but in the moment of their producing motor effects, that resolves and aspirations communicate the new 'set' to the brain.

No matter how full a reservoir of maxims one may possess, and no matter how good one's sentiments may be, if one has not taken advantage of every concrete opportunity to act, one's character may remain entirely unaffected for the better.   With good intentions, hell proverbially is paved.   This is an obvious consequence of the principles I have laid down.   A 'character,' as J.S. Mill says, 'is a completely fashioned will'; and a will, in the sense in which he means it, is an aggregate of tendencies to act in a firm and prompt and definite way upon all the principal emergencies of life.   A tendency to act only becomes effectively ingrained in us in proportion to the uninterrupted frequency with which the actions actually occur, and the brain 'grows' to their use.   When a resolve or a fine glow of feeling is allowed to evaporate without bearing practical fruit, it is worse than a chance lost: it works so as positively to hinder future resolutions and emotions from taking the normal path of discharge.   There is no more contemptible type of human character than that of the nerveless sentimentalist and dreamer, who spends his life in a weltering sea of sensibility, but never does a concrete manly deed.

This leads to a fourth maxim.   Don't preach too much to your pupils or abound in good talk in the abstract.   Lie in wait rather for the practical opportunities, be prompt to seize those as they pass, and thus at one operation get your pupils both to think, to feel, and to do.   The strokes of behavior are what give the new set to the character, and work the good habits into its organic tissue.   Preaching and talking too soon become an ineffectual bore....

...We all intend when young to be all that may become a man, before the destroyer cuts us down.   We wish and expect to enjoy poetry always, to grow more and more intelligent about pictures and music, to keep in touch with spiritual and religious ideas, and even not to let the greater philosophic thoughts of our time develop quite beyond our view. We mean all this in youth, I say; and yet in how many middle-aged men and women is such an honest and sanguine expectation fulfilled? Surely, in comparatively few; and the laws of habit show us why. Some interest in each of these things arises in everybody at the proper age; but, if not persistently fed with the appropriate matter, instead of growing into a powerful and necessary habit, it atrophies and dies, choked by the rival interests to which the daily food is given. We make ourselves into Darwins in this negative respect by persistently ignoring the essential practical conditions of our case. We say abstractly: "I mean to enjoy poetry, and to absorb a lot of it, of course. I fully intend to keep up my love of music, to read the books that shall give new turns to the thought of my time, to keep my higher spiritual side alive, etc." But we do not attack these things concretely, and we do not begin to-day. We forget that every good that is worth possessing must be paid for in strokes of daily effort. We postpone and postpone, until those smiling possibilities are dead. Whereas ten minutes a day of poetry, of spiritual reading or meditation, and an hour or two a week at music, pictures, or philosophy, provided we began now and suffered no remission, would infallibly give us in due time the fullness of all we desire. By neglecting the necessary concrete labor, by sparing ourselves the little daily tax, we are positively digging the graves of our higher possibilities. This is a point concerning which you teachers might well give a little timely information to your older and more aspiring pupils.

According as a function receives daily exercise or not, the man becomes a different kind of being in later life. We have lately had a number of accomplished Hindoo visitors at Cambridge, who talked freely of life and philosophy. More than one of them has confided to me that the sight of our faces, all contracted as they are with the habitual American over-intensity and anxiety of expression, and our ungraceful and distorted attitudes when sitting, made on him a very painful impression. "I do not see," said one, "how it is possible for you to live as you do, without a single minute in your day deliberately given to tranquillity and meditation. It is an invariable part of our Hindoo life to retire for at least half an hour daily into silence, to relax our muscles, govern our breathing, and meditate on eternal things. Every Hindoo child is trained to this form a very early age." The good fruits of such a discipline were obvious in the physical repose and lack of tension, and the wonderful smoothness and calmness of facial expression, and imperturability of manner of these Orientals. I felt that my countrymen were depriving themselves of an essential grace of character. How many American children ever hear it said by parent or teacher, that they should moderate their piercing voices, that they should relax their unused muscles, and as far as possible, when sitting, sit quite still? Not one in a thousand, not one in five thousand! Yet, from its reflex influence on the inner mental states, this ceaseless over-tension, over-motion, and over-expression are working on us grievous national harm.

I beg you teachers to think a little seriously of this matter. Perhaps you can help our rising generation of Americans toward the beginning of a better set of personal ideals.

To go back now to our general maxims, I may at last, as a fifth and final practical maxim about habits, offer something like this: Keep the faculty of effort alive in you by a little gratuitous exercise every day. That is, be systematically heroic in little unnecessary points, do every day or two something for no other reason than its difficulty, so that, when the hour of dire need draws nigh, it may find you not unnerved and untrained to stand the test. Asceticism of this sort is like the insurance which a man pays on his house and goods. The tax does him no good at the time, and possibly may never bring him a return. But, if the fire does come, his having paid it will be his salvation from ruin. So with the man who has daily inured himself to habits of concentrated attention, energetic volition, and self-denial in unnecessary things. He will stand like a tower when everything rocks around him, and his softer fellow-mortals are winnowed like chaff in the blast.

I have been accused, when talking of the subject of habit, of making old habits appear so strong that the acquiring of new ones, and particularly anything like a sudden reform or conversion, would be made impossible by my doctrine. Of course, this would suffice to condemn the latter; for sudden conversions, however infrequent they may be, unquestionably do occur. But there is no incompatibility between the general laws I have laid down and the most startling sudden alterations in the way of character. New habits can be launched, I have expressly said, on condition of there being new stimuli and new excitements. Now life abounds in these, and sometimes they are such critical and revolutionary experiences that they change a man's whole scale of values and system of ideas. In such cases, the old order of his habits will be ruptured; and if the new motives are lasting, new habits will be formed, and build up in him a new or regenerate 'nature.'

All this kind of fact I fully allow. But the general laws of habit are no wise altered thereby, and the physiological study of mental conditions still remains on the whole the most powerful ally of hortatory ethics. The hell to be indured hereafter, of which theology tells, is no worse that the hell we make for ourselves in this world by habitually fashioning our characters in the wrong way. Could the young but realize how soon they will become mere walking bundles of habit, they would give mere heed to their conduct while in the plastic state. We are spinning our own fates, good or evil, and never to be undone. Every smallest stroke of virtue or of vice leaves its never-so-little scar. The drunken Rip Van Winkle, in Jefferson's play, excuses himself for every fresh dereliction by saying, "I won't count this time!" Well, he may not count it, and a kind Heaven may not count it; but it is being counted none the less. Down among his nerve-cells and fibres the molecules are counting it, registering and storing it up to be used against him when the next temptation comes. Nothing we ever do is, in strict scientific literalness, wiped out.

Of course, this has its good side as well as its bad one. As we become permanent drunkards by so many separate drinks, so we become saints in the moral, and authorities and experts in the practical and scientific spheres, by so many separate acts and hours of work. Let no youth have any anxiety about the upshot of his education, whatever the line of it may be. If he keep faithfully busy each hour of the working day, he may safely leave the final result to itself. He can with perfect certainity count on waking up some fine morning to find himself one of the competent ones of his generation, in whatever pursuit he may have singled out. Silently, between all the details of his business, the power of judging in all that class of matter will have built itself up within him as a possession that will never pass away. Young people should know this truth in advance. The ignorance of it has probably engendered more discouragement and faint-heartedness in youths embarking on arduous careers than all other causes put together.

DISCUSSION

We see in the writing of James some very familiar viewpoints regarding the education of the child.   To begin with, James is   indirectly arguing of the importance of the parents and the teacher to take the responsibility for instilling good habits towards learning and education in the young child. Developing positive attitudes and behaviors at an early age will allow the student not only to learn material but to enjoy the process of learning.   It is fair to say a large portion of a teachers time is often spent in trying to get a student to appreciate what it is they are trying to teach.   This frustrating and time consuming process could be somewhat alleviated if most students were to enter the classroom with an open mind and a set of basic and fundamental skills taught to them at an early age.

Furthermore, James is suggesting (maxim two) that the relationship between the parent and teacher towards the student must be an ongoing endeavor.   Behaviors must be monitored and reinforced on a continual basis; one should not assume that once a student displays a good habit, the job is over.

We can also see the utility of allowing the student to receive practical and useful applications for abstract and theoretical material (maxim four).   Students all too often make comments such as "I'll never use this stuff"; with his attitude they of course see no reason to learn the material at all.   A practical demonstration of the usefulness of the subject matter may motivate them to learn.   For example, drilling students with geometrical proofs might leave them cold.   But challenging them to design a room or a building (perhaps using computer simulation) could excite them as to how essential an understanding of geometric principles is to designers and architects.   As James states, "Preaching and talking too soon become an ineffectual bore."

Finally, James is suggesting that we as teachers demonstrate enthusiasm and interest in our fields. He challenges us to not be lazy, and to undertake efforts that will keep us mentally sharp. Perhaps what he is suggesting is that we continue to improve our habits, and to serve as models of strong influence to our students. Few teachers would argue with this wisdom.

Discussion Questions

1. How does James use the metaphor of a folded sheet of paper to describe the relation of habits to the nervous system?

2. Do you agree that 99.99% of your activities are purely automatic? Why or why not?

3. Explain the following quote in your own words: "Education is for behavior, and habits are the stuff of which behavior consists."

4. How might the fourth maxim of William James be utilized in your classroom?

5. Explain James' views on procrastination. Would his suggestions be useful in your personal life? Will you practice them as a classroom teacher?

CHAPTER NINE

BOOKER T. WASHINGTON

A child of slavery would rarely be considered a candidate for educational leadership, but Booker T. Washington, through persistence, perseverance, and commitment became the leading symbol and educational spokesman for his race. His influence stretched beyond racial boundaries to change and shape the concept of education in America.

Washington was born in 1856 to Jane Ferguson, the cook for the Burroughs plantation in Franklin County, Virginia. Emancipated after the Civil War, his family moved to Milden, West Virginia where he taught himself the alphabet and attended a segregated elementary school, while working daily in the salt furnaces and coal mines to help support the family. At age seventeen he attended Hampton Institute, a school for blacks erected under the auspices of the American Missionary Association and later supported by the Virginia legislature. His experiences there influenced and shaped the direction of his professional life. Working as a janitor for his room and board, Washington studied the trade of brick-mason and graduated with honors in 1875. Later he became the secretary to the principal of Hampton, General Samual C. Armstrong who believed that industrial education would provide the moral and economic skills needed to uplift former slaves. By recognizing the dignity of work and becoming viable members of the capitalist system, Blacks would eventually be accepted as equal participants in American society. It was Armstrong's work and ideas that served to shape and define Washington's educational philosophy.

In 1881, through the solicitation of an ex-Confederate colonel, the Alabama legislature chartered a normal school for black students in Tuskegee. Washington, through the recommendation of General Armstrong, was chosen as principal. Starting with thirty students in a dilapidated shanty provided by a local Methodist church, Washington began to create a world-famous school based on his political, social, and educational viewpoint. Facing the scars of Reconstruction and the growing prevalence of Social Darwinism, if Tuskegee was to thrive, Washington's challenge and delicate task would be to achieve the cooperation of blacks, Southern whites, and Northern whites. He convinced blacks that social equality and justice would be achieved through agricultural and industrial training, creating an economic base which would allow blacks to be assimilated into American society. Through subtle manipulation and a conciliatory style, Washington won the support of conservative whites and philanthropic Northerners by overlooking their prejudices to gain popular sentiment for uplifting the black race.

Washington's ideology emphasized moral virtues, hard work, efficiency, and individual initiative as the keys of social progress which would open the door to civil rights. Struggling to overcome obstacles through self-determination provided a foundation for success. The dignity of working with one's hands and practical education in the form of trade development would result in the skills needed for acceptance. People with a talent to share would become indispensable members of the social order. Through the acquisition of material prosperity and land ownership, blacks would become recognized and rewarded.

Washington spoke of cooperative efforts and shared responsibility between the races, but felt that ultimate progress for his race depended on self-help. Racial pride, economic self-reliance, and interracial harmony were necessary for black advancement.   Washington deplored political protest and agitation as a waste of time and detrimental to the ultimate cause of social equality.

Critics, however, labeled Washington an accommodator. They believed that Washington compromised too much on racial issues and failed to demand political rights.   Many felt that emphasizing industrial training would result in virtual second-class citizenship.   Black leaders, like W. E. B. DuBois, charged Washington with repressing black viewpoints that opposed his ideology.   Ironically, Washington's critics were demanding the same things openly for which he had been secretly striving.   However, considering public opinion at the end of Reconstruction, Washington's conciliatory style and disdain for overt political activism may have been the most effective philosophy to pursue.

Washington's success at Tuskegee brought him notoriety as a public speaker.   It was his speech to the Cotton States and International Expositions in Atlanta in 1865 that made him the undisputed spokesman for blacks in America, succeeding Frederick Douglas, who had died several months earlier. Washington used his newly gained prestige and power covertly as a political activist.   While maintaining his conciliatory public posture, he worked with Presidents Roosevelt and Taft on issues of patronage distribution, organized the black vote for the Republican party, and was sought after by politicians for advice and support.   He also fought for tenant rights, fairness in jury representation, and against railroad segregation and disfranchisement.

WASHINGTON ON ACHIEVING SOCIAL EQUALITY *

Mr. President and Gentlemen of the Board of Directors and Citizens.

One-third of the population of the South is of the Negro race. No enterprise seeking the material, civil, or moral welfare of this section can disregard this element of our population and reach the highest success. I but convey to you, Mr. President and Directors, the sentiment of the masses of my race when I say that in no way have the value and manhood of the American Negro been more fittingly and generously recognized than by the managers of this magnificent Exposition at every stage of its progress. It is a recognition that will do more to cement the friendship of the two races than any occurrence since the dawn of our freedom.

Not only this, but the opportunity here afforded will awaken among us a new era of industrial progress. Ignorant and inexperienced, it is not strange that in the first years of our new life we began at the top instead of at the bottom; that a seat in Congress or the state legislature was more sought than real estate or industrial skill; that the political convention of stump speaking had more attractions than starting a dairy farm or truck garden.

A ship lost at sea for many days suddenly sighted a friendly vessel. From the mast of the unfortunate vessel was seen a signal, "Water, water; we die of thirst!" The answer from the friendly vessel at once came back, "Cast down your bucket where you are." A second time the signal, "Water, water; send us water!" ran up from the distressed vessel, and was answered, "Cast down your bucket where you are." And a

---

* **Source**: Booker T. Washington, "**Atlanta Exposition Address**", from his *Up From Slavery*, (Doubleday, Page and Co.,1901).

third and fourth signal for water was answered, "Cast down your bucket where you are." The captain of the distressed vessel, at last heeding the injunction, cast down his bucket, and it came up full of fresh, sparkling water from the mouth of the Amazon River. To those of my race who depend on bettering their condition in a foreign land or who underestimate the importance of cultivating friendly relations with the Southern white man, who is their next-door neighbor, I would say: "Cast down your bucket where you are" -- cast it down in making friends in every manly way of the people of all races by whom we are surrounded.

Cast it down in agriculture, mechanics, in commerce, in domestic service, and in the professions. And in this connection it is well to bear in mind that whatever other sins the South may be called to bear, when it comes to business, pure and simple, it is in the South that the Negro is given a man's chance in the commercial world, and in nothing is this Exposition more eloquent than in emphasizing this chance. Our greatest danger is that in the great leap from slavery to freedom we may overlook the fact that the masses of us are to live by the productions of our hands, and fail to keep in mind that we shall prosper in proportion as we learn to dignify and glorify common labour and put brains and skill into the common occupations of life; shall prosper in proportion as we learn to draw the line between the superficial and the substantial, the ornamental gewgaws of life and the useful. No race can prosper till it learns that there is as much dignity in tilling a field as in writing a poem. It is at the bottom of life we must begin, and not at the top. Nor should we permit our grievances to overshadow our opportunities.

To those of the white race who look to the incoming of those of foreign birth and strange tongue and habits for the prosperity of the South, were I permitted I would repeat what I say to my own race, "Cast down your bucket where you are." Cast it down among the eight millions of Negroes whose habits you know, whose fidelity and love you have tested in days when to have proved treacherous meant the ruin of your firesides. Cast down your bucket among these people who have, without strikes and labour wars, tilled your fields, cleared your forests, builded you railroads and cities, and brought forth treasures from the bowels of the earth, and helped make possible this magnificent representation of the progress of the south. Casting down your bucket among my people, helping and encouraging them as you are doing on these grounds, and to education of head, hand, and heart, you will find that they will buy your surplus land, make blossom the waste places in your fields, and run your factories. While doing this, you can be sure in the future, as in the past, that you and your families will be surrounded by the most patient, faithful, law-abiding, and unresentful people that the world has seen. As we have proved our loyalty to you in the past, in nursing your children, watching by the sick-bed of your mothers and fathers, and often following them with tear-dimmed eyes to their graves, so in the future, in our humble way, we shall stand by you with a devotion that no foreigner can approach, ready to lay down our lives, if need be, in defence of yours, interlacing our industrial, commercial, civil, and religious life with yours in a way that shall make the interests of both races one. In all things that are purely social we can be as separate as the fingers, yet one as the hand in all things essential to mutual progress.

There is no defence or security for any of us except in the highest intelligence and development of all. If anywhere there are efforts tending to curtail the fullest growth of the Negro, let these efforts be turned into stimulating, encouraging, and making him the most useful and intelligent citizen. Effort or means so invested will pay a thousand per cent. interest. These efforts will be twice blessed -- "blessing him that gives and him that takes."

There is no escape through law of man or God from the inevitable: --

The laws of changeless justice bind
Oppressor with oppressed;
And close as sin and suffering joined
We march to fate abreast.

Nearly sixteen millions of hands will aid you in pulling the load upward, or they will pull against you the load downward. We shall constitute one-third and more of the ignorance and crime of the South, or one-third its intelligence and progress; we shall contribute one-third to the business and industrial prosperity of the South, or we shall prove a veritable body of death, stagnating, depressing, retarding every effort to advance the body politic.

Gentlemen of the Exposition, as we present to you our humble effort at an exhibition of our progress, you must not expect overmuch. Starting thirty years ago with ownership here and there in a few quilts and pumpkins and chickens (gathered from miscellaneous sources), remember the path that has led from these to the inventions and production of agricultural implements, buggies, steam-engines, newspapers, books, statuary, carving, paintings, the management of drugstores and banks, has not been trodden without contact with thorns and thistles. While we take pride in what we exhibit as a result of our independent efforts, we do not for a moment forget that our part in this exhibition would fall far short of your expectations but for the constant help that has come to our educational life, not only from the Southern states, but especially from Northern philanthropists, who have made their gifts a constant stream of blessing and encouragement.

The wisest among my race understand that the agitation of questions of social equality is the extremest folly, and that progress in the enjoyment of all the privileges that will come to use must be the result of severe and constant struggle rather than of artificial forcing. No race that has anything to contribute to the markets of the world is long in any degree ostracized. It is important and right that all privileges of the law be ours, but it is vastly more important that we be prepared for the exercises of these privileges. The opportunity to earn a dollar in a factory just now is worth infinitely more than the opportunity to spend a dollar in an opera-house.

In conclusion, may I repeat that nothing in thirty years has given us more hope and encouragement, and drawn us so near to you of the white race, as this opportunity offered by the Exposition; and here bending, as it were, over the altar that represents the results of the struggles of your race and mine, both starting practically empty-handed three decades ago, I pledge that in your effort to work out the great and intricate problem which God has laid at the doors of the South, you shall have at all times the patient, sympathetic help of my race; only let this be constantly in mind, that while from representations in these buildings of the product of field, of forest, of forest, of mine, of factory, letters, and art, much good will come, yet far above and beyond material benefits will be that higher good, that, let us pray God, will come, in a blotting out of sectional differences and racial animosities and suspicions, in a determination to administer absolute justice, in a willing obedience among all classes to the mandates of law. This, this, coupled with our material prosperity, will bring into our beloved South a new heaven and a new earth.

DISCUSSION

This Address contains the essence of Washington's social and educational philosophy. His words speak optimistically of an American society in which all races can live with equal rights and mutual respect. Following Reconstruction, his use of ambiguous or conciliatory language served to soothe and gain support of whites, while providing hope for his own race. Blacks were encouraged to remain in the South and work to gain social justice through economic growth. Through industrial and moral training, as well as the acquisition of material prosperity, blacks would achieve their political and civil rights as equals in a capitalist society. Agitation for social equality, which would cause interracial animosity and mistrust, would only result in delaying its acquisition.

To insure the continued success of black education and progress, Washington had to address the need for cooperation and friendship between the races. Whites were encouraged to look at blacks as viable members of their society. He emphasized mutual dependence in the phrase, "In all things purely social we can be as separate as the fingers, yet one as the hand in all things essential to mutual progress." Only through the educational development of all people, black and white, to be useful, productive, and responsible citizens, can any community attain its ultimate potential. Washington's subtle manipulation of the attitudes, concerns, and fears of his generation, served to create an atmosphere that allowed for the expansion and growth of black education. He would spend the remainder of his professional career as the leading spokesman for American blacks.

Discussion Questions

1. How did Booker T. Washington's life model his educational ideology?

2. What were the racial attitudes of Americans after Reconstruction? How did attitudes vary regionally and racially?

3. What do you think were the similarities and differences between black and white schools of Washington's era?

4. What were the key factors of Washington's success as an educational leader?

5. Do you oppose or support the educational philosophy of Booker T. Washington? Defend your opinion. Would you feel differently if you were living in 1895?

CHAPTER TEN

JOHN DEWEY

The philosopher John Dewey (1859-1952) is undoubtedly
one of the most famous educators of the 20th century. His
name is recognized throughout America, though his influences
have been felt in other parts of the world; in particular, his
lectures in China and Japan made a lasting impression. Dewey's
ideas are representative of the philosophy of *pragmatism*. He,
along with C. S. Pierce and William James, was a pioneer in the
development of this distinctively American philosophical
movement. The spirit of pragmatism rests with its contention
that ideas are valuable if and only if they make a real
difference in our day to day lives. It rejects much philosophy
as either overly technical or useless. While Pierce focused
primarily on the application of pragmatism in the areas of logic
and science, and James on the discipline of psychology and such
issues as religious belief, Dewey concentrated on the more
social concerns, especially in the philosophy of education. He
was interested in social theory in general, and founded his
theories about education on the values of a *democratic* society
which, he taught, required a system of education which
promotes the sense of individual self-worth coupled with a
recognition of our membership and obligations to the society as
a whole. In his landmark book, *Democracy and Education*,
Dewey discusses the connections between educational theories
and the structure of democracy. He had a clear sense, as did
Plato, that education and social structures are interrelated and,
therefore, must be considered simultaneously.

Dewey was born in Burlington, Vermont, the son of a
shopkeeper. He was not an especially good student in primary

and secondary school. He tells us that he had no interest and found no inspiration in the strict disciplinarianism which was the style of education in his day. He did, however, work very hard in college and graduated from the University of Vermont at the age of 20. He was significantly influenced by his teachers. One excellent teacher, H.A.P. Torrey, served as Dewey's mentor before he went on to graduate school. He received the Ph.D in philosophy from John Hopkins University in 1884. He went on to teach at the Universities of Michigan and Chicago, and ended his teaching career at Columbia University.

Dewey was born during the same year that Darwin's *The Origin of Species* was published. This is interesting in light of the great influence that Darwin's ideas had on him. For it was Darwin who had demonstrated with great scientific precision that the human being is a biological organism which is *actively* engaged with its environment. And Dewey adapted a great lesson from Darwin concerning the goals of every human being, i.e., like all living creatures, we are challenged to adapt to an environment which is in constant change. What survives is successful; truth=what works!

Dewey held to a *naturalistic* philosophy of human nature. This view prefers to look at the human being as a completely natural creature (as opposed to supernatural) and chooses the scientific method as its guide. Dewey felt that the capacity for knowledge and intelligence is the distinctive feature of the human animal. And like John Locke before him, he argued the importance of investigating the nature of knowledge and intelligence because so many philosophers and scientists, in his view, had greatly misunderstood them both. In particular, Dewey was interested in dispelling a certain model of knowledge which had been proposed by the rationalists and empiricists alike. According to Dewey, this fallacious view saw the knower as analogous to the spectator looking at some object from a vantage point outside it. In his book, *Creative Intelligence*, Dewey criticizes this view that ". . . knowledge consists in surveying the world, looking at it, getting the view of a spectator." Such a view of knowledge fosters two assumptions which Dewey finds erroneous. First, it holds that the knowing subject is "outside of" and "external" to what is known. But Dewey believed that the knower is in constant interaction *with* the *environment*--the knower is involved *in* it. Secondly, the fallacious view interprets knowledge as originally a *passive reception* of ideas, whereas Dewey argued that knowing is an *active relation* to the environment. Knowledge, he argued, is based on experience, but experience involves activity, not passive receptivity. Again, in *Creative Intelligence,* he writes that "The most patient patient is more than a receptor. He is also an agent--a reactor, one trying experiments, . . . Experience, in other words, is a matter of simultaneous doings and sufferings." The knower is acting and interacting with the world. Intelligence, then, is the ability to act in relation to the environment; to adjust to it, to cope with it, in short, to survive within it. ⌊Knowledge is not a matter of "seeing" some reality which is already "there." Knowledge is an active relation which, in fact, "makes" reality.⌋ For example, if a part of the environment needs to be changed since it fosters bad habits or behaviors, knowledge and intelligence are the means of changing it.

Knowledge is, therefore, an *instrument* for change and survival. It is fitting that Dewey refers to his view as "Instrumentalism." Our capacity to think, he taught, is an instrument for change and survival within our environment. And there is nothing more important, he thought, than the role that education plays in the process. Nothing is more powerful than education as a tool for change, especially for social change.

The cornerstone of Dewey's theory of education is his belief that education should begin by mirroring what our situation actually is, i.e., we are organisms dealing with an environment. So then, education should be *experimental*, since our survival reflects an experiment with the environment--we do try many alternative ways for solving problems that we come up against in our world.   And Dewey offers the scientific method as a model for the proper way to deal with these challenges and the best foundation for education in general. The experimental nature of education, indeed, is consistent with the spirit of democracy too, which is necessarily open to workable alternatives.

If education is to be experimental then we should be very leery of bringing preconceived absolutes to the classroom. In fact Dewey rejects the style of education which is overly focused on subject-matter in general.   The "subject-matter centered" type of education, he thought, assumes that the best way to educate the young is by a uniformity of information and arrangement.   The child is seen as a passive receiver of some specified content previously deemed "essential."   It also promotes group ranking of children according to how well they accumulate the subject-matter predesigned for them.   This view is all too neat and tidy for Dewey.   And he could not help but protest against it.   For Dewey, it is the student, the young child him or herself which should be the starting point of education.   "Child-centered" education, for Dewey, is an idea he promoted while at the University of Chicago where he served as the director for the Laboratory School for children.   He preferred to see the classroom as a laboratory which allowed for creative interaction with children rather than strict, already determined outcomes.   The point of departure was the child's own interests and initiatives.

Some have criticized this idea as too permissive and lacking in discipline.   Indeed, Dewey's entire philosophy of education has been attacked, and for the most part, misunderstood.   Dewey did not promote uncontrolled and chaotic atmospheres in the classroom.   He recognized the need for control and guidance.   This is the role that the teacher must play.   But the teacher must not be simply a strict disciplinarian and "dispenser of information."   Children are not simply empty vessels waiting to be "filled" with what the teacher deems worthy.   The teacher and the child are together members of a larger society. Dewey preferred to see the relationship between the teacher and student as one of "learners together."

Teaching requires more than knowledge, it requires skill; it is an *art*. The teacher should begin with the child, all the while promoting self-awareness and a social consciousness in a playful and creative atmosphere. Learning need not be dull to be serious and important!

Dewey truly loved children. With his first wife he had six children. After her death, Dewey remarried and together with his second wife he adopted two more children; war orphans (brother and sister). Spending his last years on the family owned farm in Pennsylvania, Dewey is remembered as a truly happy and loving father and husband.

DEWEY ON SOCIETY AND EDUCATION*

ARTICLE I--WHAT EDUCATION IS

I Believe that:
--all education proceeds by the participation of the individual in the social consciousness of the race. This process begins unconsciously almost at birth, and is continually shaping the individual's powers, saturating his consciousness, forming his habits, training his ideas, and arousing his feelings and emotions. Through this unconscious education the individual gradually comes to share in the intellectual and moral resources which humanity has succeeded in getting together. He becomes an inheritor of the funded capital of civilization. The most formal and technical education in the world cannot safely depart from this general process. It can only organize it or differentiate it in some particular direction.

--the only true education comes through the stimulation of the child's powers by the demands of the social situations in which he finds himself. Through these demands he is stimulated to act as a member of a unity, to emerge from his original narrowness of action and feeling, and to conceive of himself from the standpoint of the welfare of the group to which he belongs. Through the responses which others make to his own activities he comes to know what these mean in social terms. . . . For instance, through the response which is made to the child's instinctive babblings the child comes to know what those babblings mean; they are transformed into articulate language . . . .

---

* **Source**: John Dewey, **My Pedagogic Creed**, from *The School Journal*, A Weekly Journal of Education, LIV (E. L. Kellogg & Co.January, 1897).

--this educational process has two sides--one psychological and one sociological--and that neither can be subordinated to the other, or neglected, without evil results following. Of these two sides, the psychological is the basis. The child's own instincts and powers furnish the material and give the starting-point for all education. Save as the efforts of the educator connect with some activity which the child is carrying on of his own initiative independent of the educator, education becomes reduced to a pressure from without. It may, indeed, give certain external results, but cannot be called truly educative. . . . If it chances to coincide with the child's activity it will get a leverage; if it does not, it will result in friction, or disintegration, or arrest of the child nature.

--knowledge of social conditions, of the present state of civilization, is necessary in order properly to interpret the child's powers. The child has his own instincts and tendencies, but we do not know what these mean until we can translate them into their social equivalents. We must be able to carry them back into a social past and see them as the inheritance of previous race activities. We must also be able to project them into the future to see what their outcome and end will be . . . .

--the psychological and social sides are organically related, and that education cannot be regarded as a compromise between the two, or a superimposition of one upon the other . . . .

-- . . . With the advent of democracy and modern industrial conditions, it is impossible to foretell definitely just what civilization will be twenty years from now. Hence it is impossible to prepare the child for any precise set of conditions. To prepare him for the future life means to give him command of himself; it means so to train him that he will have the full and ready use of all his capacities . . . .

In sum, I believe that the individual who is to be educated is a social individual, and that society is an organic union of individuals. If we eliminate the social factor from the child we are left only with an abstraction; if we eliminate the individual factor from society, we are left with an inert and lifeless mass.

ARTICLE II--WHAT THE SCHOOL IS

I Believe that:

--the school is primarily a social institution. Education being a social process, the school is simply that form of community life in which all those agencies are concentrated that will be most effective in bringing the child to share in the inherited resources of the race, and to use his own powers for social ends.

--education, therefore, is a process of living and not a preparation for future living.

--the school must represent present life--life as real and vital to the child as that which he carries on in the home, in the neighborhood, or on the playground.

--that education which does not occur through forms of life, forms that are worth living for their own sake, is always a poor substitute for the genuine reality, and tends to cramp and deaden.

--the school, as an institution, should simplify existing social life; should reduce it, as it were, to an embryonic form. Existing life is so complex that the child cannot be brought into contact with it without either confusion or distraction . . . .

--as such simplified social life, the school life should grow gradually out of the home life; that it should take up and continue the activities with which the child is already familiar in the home.

-- . . . this is a psychological necessity, because it is the only way of securing continuity in the child's growth, the only way of giving a background of past experience to the new ideas given in school.

--it is also a necessity because the home is the form of social life in which the child has been nurtured and in connection with which the child has had his moral training. It is the business of the school to deepen and extend his sense of values bound up in his home life.

--much of present education fails because it neglects this fundamental principle of the school as a form of community life. It conceives the school as a place where certain information is to be given, where certain lessons are to be learned, or where certain habits are to be formed. The value of these is conceived as lying largely in the remote future; the child must do these things for the sake of something else he is to do; they are mere preparations. As a result they do not become a part of the life experience of the child and so are not truly educative.

--the moral education centers upon this conception of the school as a mode of social life, that the best and deepest moral training is precisely that which one gets through having to enter into proper relations with others in a unity of work and thought. The present educational systems, so far as they destroy or neglect this unity, render it difficult or impossible to get any genuine, regular moral training.

--. . . The teacher is not in the school to impose certain ideas or to form certain habits in the child, but is there as a member of the community to select the influences which shall affect the child and assist him in properly responding to these influences.

--the discipline of the school should proceed from the life of the school as a whole and not directly from the teacher.

--the teacher's business is simply to determine, on the basis of larger experience and riper wisdom, how the discipline of life shall come to the child.

--all questions of grading of the child and his promotion should be determined by reference to the same standard. Examinations are of use only so far as they test the child's fitness for social life and reveal the place in which he can be of the most service and where he can receive the most help.

ARTICLE III--THE SUBJECT-MATTER OF EDUCATION

I Believe that:

--. . . the subject-matter of the school curriculum should mark a gradual differentiation out of the primitive unconscious unity of social life.

--we violate the child's nature and render difficult the best ethical results by introducing the child too abruptly to a number of special studies, of reading, writing, geography, etc., out of relation to this social life.

--the true center of correlation on the school subjects is not science, nor literature, nor history, nor geography, but the child's own social activities.

--. . .the primary basis of education is in the child's powers at work along the same general constructive lines as those which have brought civilization into being.

--. . . there is, therefore, no succession of studies in the ideal school curriculum. If education is life, all life has, from the outset, a scientific aspect, an aspect of art and culture, and an aspect of communication. It cannot, therefore, be true that the proper studies for one grade are mere reading and writing, and that at a later grade, reading, or literature, or science may be introduced. The progress is not in the succession of studies, but in the development of new attitudes towards, and new interests in, experience.

--education must be conceived as a continuing reconstruction of experience; that the process and the goal of education are one and the same thing . . . .

ARTICLE IV--THE NATURE OF METHOD

I Believe that:

--the question of method is ultimately reducible to the question of the order of development of the child's powers and interests. The law for presenting and treating material is the law implicit within the child's own nature. Because this is so I believe the following statements are of supreme importance as determining the spirit in which education is carried on:

--the active side precedes the passive in the development of the child-nature; that expression comes before conscious impression; that the muscular development precedes the sensory; that movements come before conscious sensations; I believe that consciousness is essentially motor or impulsive; that conscious states tend to project themselves in action.

--the neglect of this principle is the cause of a large part of the waste of time and strength in school work. The child is thrown into a passive, receptive, or absorbing attitude. The conditions are such that he is not permitted to follow the law of his nature; the result is friction and waste.

--. . . the image is the great instrument of instruction. What a child gets out of any subject presented to him is simply the images which he himself forms with regard to it.

-if nine-tenths of the energy at present directed towards making the child learn certain things were spent in seeing to it that the child was forming proper images, the work of instruction would be indefinitely facilitated . . . .

--interests are the signs and symptoms of growing power. I believe that they represent drawing capacities. Accordingly the constant and careful observation of interests is the utmost importance for the educator.

--. . . only through the continual and sympathetic observation of childhood's interests can the adult enter into the child's life and see what it is ready for, and upon what material it could work most readily and fruitfully.

--these interests are neither to be humored nor repressed. To repress interest is to substitute the adult for the child, and so to weaken intellectual curiosity and alertness, to suppress initiative, and to deaden interest. To humor the interests is to substitute the transient for the permanent . . . .

--the emotions are the reflex of actions.

--to endeavor to stimulate or arouse the emotions apart from their corresponding activities is to introduce an unhealthy and morbid state of mind.

--if we can only secure right habits of action and thought, with reference to the good, the true, and the beautiful, the emotions will for the most part take care of themselves . . . .

ARTICLE V--THE SCHOOL AND SOCIAL PROGRESS

I Believe that:

--education is the fundamental method of social progress and reform.

--all reforms which rest simply upon the enactment of law, or the threatening of certain penalties, or upon changes in mechanical or outward arrangements, are transitory and futile.

--education is a regulation of the process of coming to share in the social consciousness; and that the adjustment of individual activity on the basis of social consciousness is the only sure method of social reconstruction . . . .

--the community's duty to education is, therefore, its paramount moral duty. By law and punishment, by social agitation and discussion, society can regulate and form itself in a more or less haphazard and chance way. But through education society can formulate its own purposes, can organize its own means and resources, and thus shape itself with definiteness and economy in the direction in which it wishes to move.

--when society once recognizes the possibilities in this direction, and the obligations which these possibilities impose, it is impossible to conceive of the resources of time, attention, and money which will be put at the disposal of the educator.

--it is the business of every one interested in education to insist upon the school as the primary and most effective interest of social progress and reform in order that society may be awakened to realize what the school stands for, and aroused to the necessity of endowing the educator with sufficient equipment properly to perform his task.

--education thus conceived marks the most perfect and intimate union of science and art conceivable in human experience.

--the art of thus giving shape to human powers and adapting them to social service is the supreme art; one calling into its service the best of artists; that no insight, sympathy, tact, executive power, is too great for such service . . . .

--the teacher is engaged, not simply in the training of individuals, but in the formation of the proper social life.

--every teacher should realize the dignity of his calling; that he is a social servant set apart for the maintenance of proper social order and the securing of the right social growth.

--in this way the teacher is always the prophet of the true God and the usherer in of the true kingdom of God.

DISCUSSION

Dewey emphasizes the importance of both the psychological and social sides of education. These two are related to each other in a reciprocal fashion. Each needs the other, each need to be taken as essential aspects of education.

The starting point is "The child's own instincts and powers." But the ultimate goal is not to dispense information which will become valuable to children at some future time. The goal, rather, is for education to be involved in life itself, and in the social life of the child's world. The teacher and the child are involved in a "process of living." They are both in the "real world" now. I cannot help but feel that Dewey would reject the often heard cliche' that school prepares you for the "real world." This cliche' implies that while the student is in school, they are in some "unreal" setting. But the school is very much a part already of the real environment that we all live in.

The school is a "social institution." It is a primary source for social consciousness, progress and reform. As such, the school should be provided with sufficient resources and equipment to meet the task. So Dewey's philosophy is a strong support and message to society in general: education is not some expendable luxury, it is fundamental to any successful society. Resources spent, therefore, on education, are necessarily resources spent on society's improvement.

The teacher should not "impose" ideas and habits on children, but direct and guide the child's internal needs and desires. The child is active rather than passive. The teacher's responsibility is to give direction to the instincts of the child. And that direction should be towards "right habits of action and thought." And what are these specifically? Dewey, true to his classical philosophical roots argues that the "right" path is towards the *good*, the *true*, and the *beautiful*.

"Every teacher should recognize the dignity of his calling", writes Dewey. Without the teacher there is no education, without education there is no society--we will all, as Aristotle has said, shrivel up on the vine.

DISCUSSION QUESTIONS

1. Do you agree with Dewey's sense that education has a primarily social function?

2. Are Dewey's criticisms of "subject-matter centered" education valid? Discuss why or why not.

3. Is Dewey's support for a "child-centered" form of education workable? Do you agree with some of the criticisms leveled against it? Explain.

4. Do you support Dewey's idea that the student and teacher are "learners together"? Explain why or why not.

5. How could Dewey's ideas be reflected in the classroom? What are some creative ways his thinking could be utilized? Remember, for Dewey the classroom is a laboratory--do not be afraid to experiment!

CHAPTER ELEVEN

MARIA MONTESSORI

Maria Montessori dared to ignore the conventional wisdom of her time, becoming a doctor of medicine rather than take on the traditionally female role of teacher.

Born in 1870 in Ancona, Italy, Maria was the only child of a successful, well-educated family. She had a particularly close relationship with her mother, who encouraged Maria in every pursuit. Originally Montessori, who displayed an aptitude for mathematics, wanted to study engineering. A strong interest in biology supplanted that goal with the decision to study medicine. Despite the reaction of her father, among others, that her aspirations were outrageous, Montessori graduated as the first female Doctor of Medicine in Italy.

While working at the Psychiatric Clinic of the University of Rome, Montessori became interested in the education of retarded children. Believing, through her observation, that these children were more capable of learning than previously thought, she created the first orthophrenic school in Rome to work with these children. She became convinced that retardation should be treated as a pedagogical, rather than a medical, problem, and also that the materials and methods she developed while working with these children could be successfully employed with all children.

Montessori seized the opportunity to try out her ideas with normal children when the Association of Good Building in

San Lorenzo asked her to work with children left unsupervised during the day by their working parents. Using funds previously earmarked for repair of the children's vandalism, she opened the Casa del Bambini to the preschool children of the community. Here was a real-life laboratory enabling Montessori to develop her educational philosophy, which eventually spread throughout the world. After her work with Casa del Bambini, Montessori devoted the rest of her professional career to lecturing, writing, and defending this philosophy.

What is the essence of this philosophy?

First of all, the child is a being gifted with special abilities, particularly between birth and age six, allowing him to learn more rapidly and easily than at any other period of his life. Montessori refers to this period as the "stage of the absorbent mind," a time when the child appears to almost absorb his environment. When he is given the freedom to explore, examine, experiment and interact with the multitude of objects and situations in his environment, the child is stimulated and energized, and gains a sense of power in a period of literal self-creation.

Montessori believed that growth depended on sensitive periods of development in which a child learns in spurts. This concept countered the traditional assumption that a child learns approximately the same amount everyday. During these spurts, a child focuses on objects or tasks that serve to quench an intrinsic thirst for specific knowledge. Montessori noted that a child would concentrate extremely hard, persistently repeat actions, and exhibit self-discipline as he worked diligently toward mastering a particular activity. It was Montessori's conviction that if children are to progress successfully through these sensitive periods of development, they must be free to act on objects or tasks in their environment when their interest arises. The power of a child's internal motivation is so intense that the need to reward or punish as a means of directing or motivating a child's educational efforts is not necessary. Children, independent, free to choose, and driven to be satisfied, possess the educational direction which enables them to thrive intellectually and achieve systematic mastery of their environment.

Another crucial element of Montessori's philosophy of education is the role of teacher. A good teacher is not the infallible authority figure of the traditional classroom. Gone is the need to dominate the classroom, to administer discipline like a drill sergeant, and to orchestrate and control every aspect of a student's school day. Montessori preferred training prospective teachers that had no previous teacher preparation or experience. In this way, she could emphasize what she believed to be the essential instrument of effective teaching, observation.

Observation lies at the heart of the entire Montessori method. It was through observation and variations of the case study method that she developed her approach to teaching. She would not propose theoretical or pedagogical conclusions until, through careful observation of her students, she could objectively verify the occurrence of specific situations. Montessori emphasized that observation was the tool that enabled teachers to determine the needs and interests of their students. The teacher, instead of being quick to speak, benefits more by listening to the students to determine necessary activities, materials, and interactions to make available. This means the authority role of the instructor is replaced by that of facilitator.

As a facilitator, the teacher should become an invisible catalyst whose major responsibility is to create a learning environment that, through careful observation of student movement and behavior, meets the needs and interests of the students and allows them to develop and achieve satisfaction. The teacher should not be espousing a particular opinion or ideology, but should approach the students free of prejudice and fear. The educational opportunities provided should correspond to a child's stage of mental development and not be determined by a rigid curriculum or whim of the teacher. The learning environment should be adjusted to correspond to the children's need to develop their own nature, to become a self-directed, independent individual.

The Montessori method emphasizes that practical, sensory, and formal skills be included in the prepared learning environment of an effective classroom. Preplanned didactic materials are provided for the children to manipulate in a self-directed manner, so the child can attain mastery through individualized activity. The materials are designed to be pleasing to students, draw their attention, correspond to their movement, and reduce the number of possible mistakes, allowing for greater success. The materials address, in a holistic nature, the child's physical, mental, and moral aspects. Certain materials promote competence in practical life skills which liberate the child by enabling him/her to independently handle ordinary tasks such as getting dressed and undressed, serving a meal, washing dishes, and displaying proper manners. The child achieves sensory development and muscular coordination through repetition of exercises. The child then proceeds at a rapid pace, almost like an explosion, into the development of the formalized skills of reading, writing, and mathematics.

Throughout this learning process, the teacher does not act as an instructor in the usual sense, but rather facilitates learning through didactic materials in a prepared environment. By doing this, the teacher has provided the means for growth and development without dictating direction to the students. This form of auto-education in which the student chooses his own experiences does not mean that the teacher becomes a useless bystander. To the contrary, the teacher must have a personality that allows for a relationship with the student that is conducive to interaction and contact when the child feels the need. Montessori emphasized that teachers should possess training in child psychology which would enable them to respect the individual nature of each child and refrain from normative comparisons. By providing experiences that address internal drives, determining proper moments to encourage, and most importantly by refraining from external direction or intervention, the teacher allows children to develop the maximum potential of their individual nature.

MONTESSORI: MY SYSTEM OF EDUCATION*

My system is to be considered a system leading up, in a general way, to education. It can be followed not only in the education of little children from three to six years of age, but can be extended to children up to ten years of age. It is not a simple theory, but has been experimented with and put into practice. Its results constitute a scientific proof of its value.

Altho the first part of my experiment deals only with children between the ages of three and six years, nevertheless it must be considered as a "directive system" for the education of all children having attained the school age. In fact, my last experiments, not yet known to the public, have been made on children up to ten years of age, and the same directive system has proven satisfactory. The results were of still higher importance than in the first case with smaller children because richer in practical evidence both in the formation of character and in the attainment of knowledge.

The fact on which it was possible to establish my system is the psychologic fact of the "attention" of the child, intensively chained to any exterior object or fact, which proves in the child a spontaneous, altho complex activity of its entire little personality.

It will be of some interest to relate here the episode that made me decide to plan out a special method for the education of children.

I was making the first experiments in San Lorenzo (Roma), trying to apply my principles and part of the material

* **Source**: Maria Montessori, "**My System of Education**", in the *Journal of Proceedings and Addresses of the Fifty-Third Annual Meeting and International Congress of Education, 4,* 1915.

that I had previously used in the education of backward children.

A little girl, about three years of age, was deeply absorbed in the work of placing wooden blocks and cylinders in a frame for that purpose. The expression of her face was that of such intense attention, that it was almost a revelation to me. Never before had I seen a child look with such "fixedness" upon an object, and my conviction about the instability of attention which goes incessantly from one thing to another, a fact which is so characteristic in little children, made the phenomenon the more remarkable to me.

I watched the child without interrupting her, and counted how many times she would do her work over and over. It seemed that she was never going to stop. As I saw that it would take a very long time, I took the little armchair on which she was sitting and placed child and chair on the big table. Hastily she put the frame across the chair, gathered blocks and cylinders in her lap, and continued her work undisturbed. I invited the other children to sing, but the little girl went on with her work and continued even after the singing had ceased. I counted forty-four different exercises which she made, and when she finally stopped, and did so absolutely independently from an exterior cause that could disturb her, she looked around with an expression of great satisfaction, as if she were awakening from a deep and restful sleep.

The impression I received from the observation was that of a discovery. The same phenomenon became very common among those children, and it was noticed in every school in every country where my system was introduced; therefore it can be considered as a constant reaction which takes place in connection with certain exterior conditions that can be well established. Each time a similar "polarization" of the attention occurred, the child began to transmute itself completely; it became calmer, more expressive, more intelligent, and evidenced extraordinary interior qualities, which recalled the phenomena of the highest mentality. When the phenomenon of polarization of the attention had occurred, all that was confused and drifting in the conscience of the child seemed to assume a form, the marvelous characters of which were reproduced in each individual.

This reminded one of the life of man that may be scattered indiscriminately in a chaotic condition, until a special object attracts it and gives it a fixed form, and then only is man revealed unto himself and begins to live. This spiritual phenomenon, which may coinvolve the whole conscience of the adult, is therefore but one of the ever-present aspects of the "formation of the inner life." It is met with as a normal beginning of the inner life of children, and it follows the development so as to come within the reach of research as an experimental fact.

It was thus that the soul of the child gave its revelations, and, guided by these revelations, there arose a method where spiritual liberty became demonstrated.

The news of this fact rapidly spread thruout the world, and it was received at first as a miracle. Then little by little, as the experiments were repeated among the most diverse races, the simplicity and evidence of the principles of this spiritual treatment were recognized.

When you have solved the problem of controlling the attention of the child, you have solved the entire problem of its education. The importance of a scheme to concentrate the attention is self-evident. Professor William James, the renowned authority on psychology in America, points out to us how there exists in children that exterior variability of attention that makes it so difficult to give them the first lessons. The reflective and passive character of the attention, by which the child seems to belong less to itself than to any object that may attract its attention, is the first thing that the teacher must conquer. The ability incessantly to recall a wandering and scattered attention, always ready to vanish, is the real root of judgment, character, and will; that system of education that succeeds in bringing this faculty to the highest degree should be the ideal and standard system.

To be able to choose objects that will interest and hold the attention of the child is to know the means of aiding it in its mental development. All things which naturally arise and hold the attention with considerable steadiness are those which represent a "necessity" for the child. Toward these things its attention is directed in a natural, almost instinctive way. All other things that attract its attention do so only lightly, transitorily, and for a very short period of time. Thus the newborn child has a series of unco-ordinate movements, but the complex movement of sucking, which is in direct proportion to its need of food, is performed with regularity, co-ordination, and steadiness. We must recognize that something like this is needed for its psychic development.

Consider the little girl only three years of age who performs the same exercise fifty times. A crowd is reaming about her, a piano is playing, a chorus is sung, and nothing can distract her from her deep concentration. In a similar way, the baby holds on to the breast of the mother without being interrupted by any exterior agent and lets go only after its need is satisfied.

How shall we choose the means of development by experiments? Since a constant and peculiar psychic reaction is an established fact, it is possible to determine some stimulating (reactive) agents or objects that can aid the spontaneous development. The character of this reaction itself must be the guide to the choice of these objects which are to constitute the implements or tools for this scientific work.

Each one of these instruments must be built with every detail to answer the purpose. As the lenses of the optician are made in accordance with the laws of refraction, the pedagogical instrument must be chosen to correspond exactly to the psychic manifestations of the child.

Such an instrument could be compared to a systematized mental test. It is not, however, established as an external criterion of measurement with the purpose of estimating the instantaneous psychic reaction which it produces, but on the contrary it is a stimulus which must be determined by the psychic reactions which it is capable of producing and maintaining in a permanent manner. It is the psychic reaction which determines and establishes the systematic mental test and the psychic reaction which serves as the sole means of comparison in determining the tests. It is a polarization of the attention and the repetition of the acts to which it corresponds. When a stimulus corresponds in this way to the reflex personality, it serves, not to measure, but to maintain an active reaction. Therefore it is a stimulus of inner formation. In fact, it is upon such activity, aroused and maintained, that the associative organism begins its inner elaborations in relation to the stimuli.

It is not as a scale for weighing personality that this science comes into the old sphere of pedagogy as it was in the case of the experimental psychology introduced in the school up to the present time. It is a science intended for the purpose of "transforming" personality, thus taking the place of a true and real pedagogy. While old pedagogy in all its different interpretations had for its point of view and starting-base the conception of a "receptive personality," which was supposed to receive tuition and allow itself to be passively transformed, this scientific direction presupposes an active personality, reflective and associative, whose activity manifests itself thru a series of reactions derived from systematic stimuli chosen by experiments. This new "pedagogy" belongs therefore to the series of modern sciences not of old speculations. But the method that embodies it, that is to say the attempt, observation, retrying, taking notice of new phenomena, the reproduction of said phenomena and utilizing them, places this new pedagogy among the experimental sciences.

Nothing is more interesting than these experiments. By them we can establish, with the greatest precision, all necessary exterior stimuli definite in their qualities and quantity. Small frames, for instance, of different forms, arouse only a temporary and transient attention in a child three years of age; but, gradually enlarging the size of the frames, you will reach that limit at which the attention is steadily held, the activity stimulated by them will be permanent, and the exercise set up in it becomes a factor of development. The experiment is repeated on several children and we come to the point where we can establish the right size of a series of objects; in the same way you can proceed to determine the color and all other qualities of your material. In order that a quality be "felt" so intensely as to hold the attention, a sufficient size and intensity are required in the stimulus. These can be determined by the degree of psychic reaction in the child in the same way that you establish which is the smallest size of colored surface which can attract the attention of the child upon the colored tablets, and so forth. The quality, then, is determined by the psychic experiment and the activity that it provokes in the child, who remains absorbed for a considerable length of time working on the same subject. It is while in this state that the phenomenon of interior development and auto-formation takes place.

Of the qualities of the objects one must be picked out which stimulates principally the highest activities of the intelligence; this is the quality that enables the child to verify mistakes. In order to create a process of auto-education, it is not sufficient that the stimulus arouses an activity, it must at the same time direct it; the child must not only be occupied for a long time on an exercise, but it must continue on it without making mistakes.

All the physical or intrinsic qualities of the objects must be determined aside from the immediate reaction of attention provoked in the child, also this fundamental characteristic of permitting the control of error, that is, to summon the active collaboration of high activities, such as comparison and judgment. For example, one of the first objects which attracts the attention of the three-year-old child, the solid insets (a series of little cylinders of various dimensions which are taken out and replaced), contains the most mechanical control, because in making one mistake in the replacing of the cylinders, one of them is left without a place. Hence a mistake is an obstacle which can be surmounted only by correction, otherwise the exercise can proceed no farther. Furthermore, the correction is so easy that the child accomplishes it by himself. The little problem which has unexpectedly sprung up before the child like a jack-in-the-box has interested him.

It may be noted, however, that the problem which has arisen is not of itself a stimulus to the interest -- does not urge the child on to the repetition of the act, or to progress. That which interests the child is not only the sense of handling the objects, but the conscious acquisition of a new power of discrimination, that of recognizing the difference of dimensions among the cylinders, the difference which at first he did not perceive. The problem arises only in relation to the mistake -- it does not accompany the normal process of development. An interest simply stimulated by curiosity in the problem would not be that formative interest which draws its sources from the needs of life itself and which, therefore, directs the construction of the inner personality. If it were only the problem which led the soul along, it might lose its own spontaneous order as every other external cause which strives to lead life astray on false paths.

On the other hand, the experimental criterion for determining the number of objects is quite different. When the instruments have been constructed with great precision, they provoke an auto-exercise so orderly and responding to the facts of inner development in such a way that at a certain point a new psychic picture is revealed, a sort of upper plane in the complete development.

Then the child spontaneously abandons the objects, but not with signs of fatigue, altho he is carried along by new energy and his mind is capable of abstraction. At this stage of development the child turns his attention to the external world and observes it in an orderly manner, according to the order which has been formed in his mind along with the preceding development, and he unconsciously begins to make a series of measured and logical comparisons which represents a real spontaneous acquisition of knowledge. This is the stage henceforth known as the Period of Discovery, discovering which evokes in the child enthusiasm and joy.

This higher stage of development is most fruitful because of its later growth. It is necessary that the child's attention should not be detained on these objects when the delicate phenomenon of abstraction begins. For example: The teachers who should at such a moment call the child to renew his activity with the objects would in so doing retard his spontaneous development, would put an obstacle in his path. When that enthusiasm which leads the child to uplift himself and to experience so many intellectual emotions is spent, then one road to progress is closed. The same mistake may be made thru an overabundance of material since it may distract the attention, may cause the use of the material to become mechanical, and may cause the child to pass by his psychological moment without seizing it or even being aware of it. These extra objects (materials) are useless and amid them the soul may lose itself. What must be accurately determined is how much material is necessary and sufficient to respond to the needs of the inner life in its development. The observation of the child's expression and of the manifestations of his activities as a whole are the guiding factors in determining the quantity.

Perhaps I insist too much on this point in order to reply to the many important objections and suggestions which have been made to me, because there are those who think that the form alone of the problem is able to arouse the interest.

In the second series of objects used to educate the eye to dimensions, the control of the error is not mechanical but psychological. The child himself, since his eye is already taught to recognize differences of dimension, will see the error if only the objects are of fixed dimensions and highly colored. For this reason the succeeding objects contain a control of error in their very size and vivid colorings. A control of error of quite a different kind and of a much higher order is found in the material used for the multiplication table where the control consists in comparing the work itself with the answer, a comparison which necessitates a marked effort of the child's intellect and will and which henceforth places him amid true conditions of a conscious auto-education. The seeming distraction is revealed in its real essence by the happy expression of the children's serious faces animated by the keenest joy. The child, to all appearances, does nothing, but only for a minute; shortly he will speak and will tell us what is taking place within him and then an outburst of activity will carry him on a round of continuous explorations and discoveries. He is saved.

On the other hand, here are other children who experience the same primitive phenomena, but they were surrounded with too many objects. At the moment of maturity they felt themselves seized, forced, actually "bound with cords" to earth. A diminution of the intensity of the attention given to new objects, instability, and hence weariness are made manifest by the cessation of inner activity. The child gives way to lower tendencies, foolish laughter, and disorderly acts. He asks for more objects and still more objects, because he has remained imprisoned in the "vicious whirl of vanities" and he no longer feels the need of gaining relief from his ennui. Such is also the fate of an adult who, in life's chaos has committed a like error -- he becomes undisciplined, weak, and "is in danger of losing himself." If someone does not help him and, tearing away all unnecessary objects, point out to him "his heaven," it will be difficult for him to have the energy to attain it by himself.

These two extreme types give an idea of the criteria by which one determines in an experiment the "quantity" of the objects used for development. The "too much" weakens and retards progress. This has been proven again and again by all my collaborators. If, on the other hand, the material is insufficient and the natural auto-exercises are unable to lead up to that state of maturity which raises one, there is no outburst of that spontaneous phenomenon of abstraction which is the second step in that auto-education which goes forward in infinite progression.

This same fundamental phenomenon of intense and prolonged attention leading to a repetition of acts guides one in finding the stimuli which are suitable to the child's age. A stimulus which causes a child of three to repeat an act forty times in succession may cause another child of six to repeat the same act only ten times; the object which quickens the interest of the three-year-old cannot quicken the interest of the six-year-old child. However, the child of six is capable of far greater attention than the three-year-old, when the stimulus is in direct relation to his activity. If the child of three has a maximum power of repetition, say of forty times in succession, the six-year-old is able to repeat an act in which he is interested two hundred times. If in the case of a three-year-old child the maximum period of continuous work on the same object is half an hour, for the six-year-old it may be more than two hours.

Thus tests give positive psychic characteristics which can almost be measured according to age. Analogously, since there are for the various ages materials for progressive development upon which the various personalities can react differently, it is possible to determine with scientific precision the level of the average psychical development according to age, a precision which I consider the famous Binet and Simon tests are far from attaining. A relationship is established between the inner needs and the stimuli.

This is a suggestion, however incomplete and insufficient, of the "possibility" of experimentally determining the means for psychic development. They can really be established and with such precision as to bring into existence a real relationship between the inner needs and the stimuli, just as there exists a relationship of form between the insect and the flower. That is to say, there remains in the organization of the external means for inner development "a material imprint," and this is that of which the soul has need in its path, in its course, in its flights. The material part does not contain the imprint of the whole soul, as the imprint of the foot does not give the imprint of the whole body, as the aviation field is not the place for the extensive course of an aeroplane, but is only a piece of terra firma necessary for the flight, and is also the resting-place, the refuge, the shed to which the aeroplane must always return. Thus, in the psychic formation, there is a material part necessary in order that the spirit may lift itself, and there the spirit must seek support, rest, and refuge. Without this, it cannot grow and rise "freely."

In order that this material may be a real support, it must reproduce and contain within itself those forms which correspond to the needs of material help. Thus, for example, in the first part of the psychic life, the material corresponds to the primitive exercising of the senses and is determined in quality and quantity by the sensorial needs supplied by nature, corresponding to the exercise of the activity sufficient in order to mature a superior psychic state of observation and abstraction. Vice versa, nothing in the material corresponds to the successive course thru the world which the infantile spirit completes with such rapture, making great acquisitions of knowledge. Then we see the spirit crying out for exercises of a higher order and behold the same primitive phenomenon of the attention, which henceforth is exercised on the alphabet and on the material for arithmetic, repeating in a more complex form the methodical exercises of the intellect, by correlating the auditory impressions with the visual and motor impressions in the written and spoken work and in the positive study of quantity, proportions, and number. Then the same accompanying phenomena are manifested which are the concomitants of patience, of constancy, and, at the same time, of vivacity and joy, and characteristic of the spirit when the inner energy has found its outlet. The field in which it can exercise itself comfortably and quietly enlarges and the spirit which becomes organized in such a way under the guidance of an order which responds to its natural order, becomes strong, grows flourishingly, and manifests itself in equilibrium, serenity, and calm, which then gives that wonderful discipline characteristic of the conduct of our children.

The practical consequences of such a system of education are: the easy and spontaneous solution of pedagogical problems considered impossible to solve; the realization of ideals thought to be utopian.

From such a system there comes forth a school where the children work for themselves -- that is, they are free. In this freedom they work much more than heretofore has been customary in school, not alone without fatigue, but with renewed nervous forces, and they attain culture more rapidly and more efficaciously--that is, they surpass the ordinary level. In fact, children can learn to read and write at four and one-half years of age generally, and in the elementary schools they save from one to two years. This educational problem, which today science propounds, is solved, tho it was considered among the insoluble questions such as the fourth dimension, perpetual motion, and the squaring of a circle. The problem is to lessen effort and at the same time increase output. In fact, the overworking of pupils has forced hygiene to insist on less work, whereas social progress requires that the schools produce men even more cultured.

Furthermore, children brought up under our method acquire a salient personality, a peculiar formation of character, and they are capable of perfect discipline, a thing which solves the problem of liberty. For liberty, as it has been tried up to now, brought about either disorder and lack of discipline or a lessening of scholarship. In truth the solution of the question of freedom depends entirely on finding the means which will serve as an aid to spontaneous psychic development, to character and to intellectual culture. In this manner auto-education is also attained, a thing which is impossible unless we determine with precision the means necessary for the child to educate himself -- that is, to develop his own activities.

Finally, in such a way is a true positive science of education initiated, which up to the present has not been given by pedagogical anthropology nor by German experimental psychology with its applications to the school in the branch called "scientific pedagogy." Such sciences have studied the personality of the pupil but have not changed it, they have pointed out and analyzed the errors of the school, but they have not reconstructed. Besides, if from these sciences there had really arisen a scientific pedagogy capable of transforming man, as the other positive sciences have transformed the environment, it would not have left educators and the public so indifferent; would have aroused a popular interest since children and the schools are of common interest to all mankind.

The scientific pedagogy, and understood thus far, does not indeed present anything but the ideal for establishing pedagogy on the lines of positive and experimental science in accordance with the progress of the time and not the realization of such an ideal. In fact, the scientific laboratory of experimental pedagogy cannot be other than the school itself, where the children live and are transformed. I believe that my system of education is founding this laboratory where the first germs of a science of man are visible because of the precision of systematic means, and also because of the effect upon human development.

DISCUSSION

Montessori describes her method of education as a "directive system." She changed the title of teacher to what she believed was a more descriptive title, that of directress. Although the child's intellectual development is self-directed, the directress has the enormous responsibility of creating a learning environment that is conducive to that development. The primary function of this environment is to gain and maintain the student's attention, thus activating the learning process.

To capture a student's attention, objects must be created and placed in the environment that will arouse interest and action. These objects must correspond to the individual nature of children, allowing them to react almost instinctively. The directress must attempt to provide sufficient quality and quantity of external stimuli suitable to satisfy the internal drives and maintain motivation of the individual student.

Through concentration and manipulation of these objects, children meet their needs and achieve inner-development. Once fulfillment of this stage has taken place, children abandon the objects of interest and turn their attention to the external world. At this time, children's minds are capable of abstraction which is the stage of auto-education that progresses in an infinite manner. The imperative of Montessori's method is the addressing of individual needs. The children are motivated to participate in what interests them. They are free to explore their environment in an effort to achieve their individual potential. This freedom of self-direction creates within the child a personality and self-discipline which eliminates the need for traditional classroom management.

Montessori contends that her philosophy of education is grounded in scientific methodology. She emphasizes, however, that educational change can not take place through scientific pedagogy that is removed from the school. To the contrary, Montessori speaks to the necessity of the school as the laboratory for change, where observation and experimentation will reveal the keys to transforming human education.

Discussion   Questions

1. How does Montessori's view of the child differ from other commonly held views?

2. How does the traditional conception of the classroom teacher differ from Montessori's directress?

3. Do you think that Montessori's "directive system" is too rigid and confining or is it too unstructured and lacking in control? Explain.

4. Do you feel that Montessori's claim of student self-discipline is realistic or overstated?   Why?

5. If you were to be appointed to a Montessori school, what objects would you bring to a productive learning environment? Do you think they would differ from the didactic materials Montessori developed?

CHAPTER TWELVE

CARL RANSOM ROGERS

As we pointed out in the introductory chapter, the fields of philosophy, psychology, and education are in part organized under the various schools of thought within each domain. The position to which we now turn our attention is usually referred to as the Humanistic perspective in Psychology, and like all other perspectives, has a number of outstanding men and women that adhere to its philosophy. Among modern psychologists Carl Rogers stands out as one of the leading founders of this movement, and as one of the most highly regarded practitioners within it.

Born in 1902 in a suburb of Chicago, Carl Ransom Rogers was the fourth of six children within the Fundamentalist Protestant family. While both of his parents were loving and caring, it is clear that they held a tight reign on their children, accepting nothing short of strict obedience to the religious and work ethics they saw as correct. Carl was not allowed to socialize outside of the family, and perhaps to remove any temptation along these lines, the family moved to a farm just outside the city, where Carl was essentially isolated. In his own words, "we did not dance, play cards, attend movies, smoke, drink, or show any sexual interest."

Carl was an avid reader, and moving to the farm stimulated his interest in farming matters.   He read all about the scientific aspects of farming, and took a strong interest in the care and rearing of farm animals.   It was natural that he would want to further his knowledge, so at age 18 he enrolled at the University of Wisconsin, majoring in agriculture. However, like many other college students, his interests changed, and he shifted from agriculture to the helping professions.   For a short time he considered joining the clergy, but finally came to realize that psychology was what he really wanted to study.   During his junior year at Wisconsin, Rogers was chosen to attend a six month World Student Christian Federation Conference in China, which was to be a major turning point in his life.   For the first time he was away from the influence of his family.   Being so far removed geographically gave him the courage to listen to his instincts and to trust his own judgements, which in some ways were very different from those of his family.   He never forgot the value of being true to oneself, and eventually incorporated this as a basic tenent in both his theory of human nature and his treatment   techniques.

Rogers returned to Wisconsin, graduating in 1924, and shortly afterward married Helen Elliott.   The Rogers had two children during their happy marriage, a son and a daughter. Rogers continued his graduate work at Columbia Teachers College in New York, receiving his Ph.D in 1929.   His first professional position was as a child guidance counselor in New York, where he became acquainted with many reputable psychiatrists schooled in the Freudian tradition.   As he worked more and more with the young people in the clinic, he began to question the value of Freudian methods, and at the same time began to formulate alternative possibilities for treatment.   In 1940, he accepted a professorship at the Ohio State University, and in 1945 returned to his native Chicago to teach at the University, where he remained until 1957.   His final formal teaching appointment was at the University of Wisconsin. During these years Rogers formalized his humanistic ideas, publishing several books and articles. In 1963 he moved to California and founded the Center for Studies of the Person. He continued to practice psychotherapy and to interact with enthusiastic students from all over the world. Carl Rogers died on February 4, 1987 of cardiac arrest.

Carl Rogers is best remembered as the originator of an approach to psychotherapy known as Client Centered Therapy. He later came to change the name to Person Centered Therapy, reflecting his belief that the basic technique in the therapeutic relationship could also be beneficially applied in a number of other settings, most notably within the school and the family. It is therefore important that we examine the basic postulates of his approach.

Person Centered Therapy is an optimistic attempt to allow an individual to accept and feel good about himself. Rogers points out that a common denominator in almost all of his clients was a low feeling of self worth. Many in fact were living lives designed to please other significant people (parents, bosses, teachers, spouses), yet they themselves were not happy. Most expressed a fear that should they speak up, live and do as they saw best, that these important people in their lives would reject them. Thus, it was a fear of rejection from others that kept them in their unhappy state. In short, they did not trust their own feelings and beliefs; they were not true to themselves. Rogers recognized this as a splitting of what he called the actual self (our own unbiased impression of our self) and the ideal self (the self we really want to be). This discongruency of the actual and ideal selves invariably led to low self esteem and low self regard. How then can this be rectified?

Rogers began with the assumption that people have an innate tendency to actualize themselves. What he means by this is the desire to grow, to achieve to the best of ones capabilities, and to realize all of ones potential. Individuals who are encouraged by their parents, and most importantly are accepted regardless of their success or failure grow up with an internal sense of positive self-regard. Because they are accepted by significant others without conditions attached, they accept themselves and are open to new and challenging experiences. This is the converse of the unhappy discongruent individual mentioned previously. Thus, for Rogers the acceptance of an individual by important others without reservation or conditions is crucial for the formation of a well adjusted competent person. Since parents and teachers are the two most influential sources in the lives of most children, sound parenting and teaching practices are absolutely necessary. For the teacher, this means a shift away from standard punitive methods to more growth enhancing techniques.

In an ideal setting the student is motivated to learn, actually wants to learn, rather than being forced to submit to the demands of a powerful authority. Rogers himself makes the following suggestions:

1. Do away with mandatory teaching. People would get together if they wanted to learn.

2. Do away with examinations, grades and credits.

3. The use of self discovered, self appropriated methods of learning.

4. The removal of traditional teaching methods, which cause the individual to distrust his own experiences, and to stifle learning.

These are powerful statements. They certainly go contrary to the typical American educational protocol. Even so, Rogers asserts that significant learning (that is, learning which influences behavior, attitudes and overall personality, as opposed to a simple accumulation of facts) is possible, and most especially with the assistance of a qualified teacher, or facilitator to use his term. This individual would possess the same characteristics as an effective Person Centered Psychotherapist. Rogers has spent years outlining these features. In short, they involve the genuineness of the teacher, the acceptance of the student by the teacher regardless of grades, talents, or personal mannerisms, an ability to empathize with the needs of the student, and the ability to relate information in a way that is meaningful to the student.

The following article is taken from Rogers text, *O n Becoming A Person*. In this reading Rogers compares the individual interacting with a therapist to the student interacting with a teacher. Both the client in therapy and the student in the classroom are engaged in a journey of self discovery, one that can best be accomplished by a warm, caring and genuine facilitator. The result in both cases is growth, fulfillment, and internal positive self regard.

ROGERS ON BECOMING A PERSON*

Presented here is a thesis, a point of view, regarding the implications which psychotherapy has for education. It is a stand which I take tentatively, and with some hesitation. I have many unanswered questions about this thesis. But it has, I think, some clarity in it, and hence it may provide a starting point from which clear differences can emerge.

Significant Learning in Psychotherapy

Let me begin by saying that my long experience as a therapist convinces me that significant learning is facilitated in psychotherapy, and occurs in that relationship. By significant learning I mean learning which is more than an accumulation of facts. It is learning which makes a difference -- in the individual's behavior, in the course of action he chooses in the future, in his attitudes and in his personality. It is a pervasive learning which is not just an accretion of knowledge, but which interpenetrates with every portion of his existence.

Now it is not only my subjective feeling that such learning takes place. This feeling is substantiated by research. In client-centered therapy, the orientation with which I am most familiar, and in which the most research has been done, we know that exposure to such therapy produces learnings, or changes, of these sorts:

The person comes see himself differently.

He accepts himself and his feelings more fully.

He becomes more self-confident and self-directing.

He becomes more the person he would like to be.

---

* **Source**: Carl Rogers, **On Becoming a Person**: A Therapist's View of Psychotherapy (Boston: Houghton Mifflin, 1961). Reprinted by permission.

He becomes more flexible, less rigid, in his perceptions.
He adopts more realistic goals for himself.
He behaves in a more mature fashion.
He changes his maladjustive behaviors, even such a long-established one as chronic alcoholism.
He becomes more acceptant of others.
He becomes more open to the evidence, both to what is going on outside of himself, and to what is going on inside of himself.
He changes in his basic personality characteristics, in constructive ways.
I think perhaps this is sufficient to indicate that these are learnings which are significant, which do make a difference.

Significant Learning in Education

I believe I am accurate in saying that educators too are interested in learnings which make a difference. Simple knowledge of facts has its value. To know who won the Battle of Poltava, or when the umpteenth opus of Mozart was first performed, may win $64,000 or some other sum for the possessor of this information, but I believe educators in general are a little embarrassed by the assumption that the acquisition of such knowledge constitutes education. Speaking of this reminds me of a forceful statement made by a professor of agronomy in my freshman year in college. Whatever knowledge I gained in his course has departed completely, but I remember how, with World War I as his background, he was comparing factual knowledge with ammunition. He wound up his little discourse with the exhortation, "Don't be a damned ammunition wagon; be a rifle!" I believe most educators would share this sentiment that knowledge exists primarily for use.

To the extent then that educators are interested in learnings which are functional, which make a difference, which pervade the person and his actions, then they might well look to the field of psychotherapy for leads or ideas. Some adaptation for education of the learning process which takes place in psychotherapy seems like a promising possibility.

The Conditions of Learning in Psychotherapy

Let us then see what is involved, essentially, in making possible the learning which occurs in therapy. I would like to spell out, as clearly as I can, the conditions which seem to be present when this phenomenon occurs.

Facing a Problem

The client is, first of all, up against a situation which he perceives as a serious and meaningful problem. It may be that he finds himself behaving in ways in which he cannot control, or he is overwhelmed by confusions and conflicts, or his marriage is going on the rocks, or he finds himself unhappy in his work. He is, in short, faced with a problem with which he has tried to cope, and found himself unsuccessful. He is therefore eager to learn, even though at the same time he is frightened that what he discovers in himself may be disturbing. Thus one of the conditions nearly always present is an uncertain and ambivalent desire to learn or to change, growing out of a perceived difficulty in meeting life.

What are the conditions which this individual meets when he comes to a therapist? I have recently formulated a theoretical picture of the necessary and sufficient conditions which the therapist provides, if constructive change or significant learning is to occur. This theory is currently being tested in several of its aspects by empirical research, but it must still be regarded as theory based upon clinical experience rather than proven fact. Let me describe briefly the conditions which it seems essential that the therapist should provide.

Congruence

If therapy is to occur, it seems necessary that the therapist be, in the relationship, a unified, or integrated, or congruent person. What I mean is that within the relationship he is exactly that he *is* -- not a facade, or a role, or a pretense. I have used the term "congruence" to refer to this accurate matching of experience with awareness. It is when the therapist is fully and accurately aware of what he is experiencing at this moment in the relationship, that he is fully congruent. Unless this congruence is present to a considerable degree it is unlikely that significant learning can occur.

Though this concept of congruence is actually a complex one, I believe all of us can recognize it in an intuitive and commonsense way in individuals with whom we deal. With one individual we recognize that he not only means exactly what he says, but that his deepest feelings also match what he is expressing. Thus whether he is angry or affectionate or ashamed or enthusiastic, we sense that he is the same at all levels -- in what he is experiencing at an organismic level, in his awareness at the conscious level, and in his words and communications. We furthermore recognize that he is acceptant of his immediate feelings. We say of such a person that we know "exactly where he stands." We tend to feel comfortable and secure in such a relationship. With another person we recognize that what he is saying is almost certainly a front or a facade. We wonder what he *really* feels, what he is really experiencing, behind this facade. We may also wonder if *he* knows what he really feels, recognizing that he may be quite unaware of the feelings he is actually experiencing. With such a person we tend to be cautious and wary. It is not the kind of relationship in which defenses can be dropped or in which significant learning and change can occur.

Thus this second condition for therapy is that the therapist is characterized by a considerable degree of congruence in the relationship. He is freely, deeply, and acceptantly himself, with his actual experience of his feelings and reactions matched by an accurate awareness of these feelings and reactions as they occur and as they change.

Unconditional Positive Regard
A third condition is that the therapist experiences a warm caring for the client -- a caring which is not possessive, which demands no personal gratification. It is an atmosphere which simply demonstrates "I care"; not "I care for you *if* you behave thus and so." Standal has termed this attitude "unconditional positive regard," since it has no conditions of worth attached to it. I have often used the term "acceptance" to describe this aspect of the therapeutic climate. It involves as much feeling of acceptance for the client's expression of negative, "bad," painful, fearful, and abnormal feelings as for his expression of "good," positive, mature, confident and social feelings. It involves an acceptance of and a caring for the client as a *separate* person, with permission for him to have his own feelings and experiences, and to find his own meanings in them. To the degree that the therapist can provide this safety-creating climate of unconditional positive regard, significant learning is likely to take place.

An Empathic Understanding
The fourth condition for therapy is that the therapist is experiencing an accurate, empathic understanding of the client's world as seen from the inside. To sense the client's private world as if it were your own, but without ever losing the "as if" quality -- this is empathy, and this seems essential to therapy. To sense the client's anger, fear, or confusion as if it were your own, yet without your own anger, fear, or confusion getting bound up in it, is the condition we are endeavoring to describe. When the client's world is this clear to the therapist, and he moves about in it freely, then he can both communicate his understanding of what is clearly known to the client and can also voice meanings in the client's experience of which the client is scarcely aware. That such penetrating empathy is important for the therapy is indicated

by Fiedler's research in which items such as the following place high in the description of relationships created by experienced therapists:

The therapist is well able to understand the patient's feelings.

The therapist is never in any doubt about what the patient means.

The therapist's remarks fit in just right with the patient's mood and content.

The therapist's tone of voice conveys the complete ability to share the patient's feelings.

Fifth Condition

A fifth condition for significant learning in therapy is that the client should experience or perceive something of the therapist's congruence, acceptance, and empathy. It is not enough that these conditions exist in the therapist. They must, to some degree, have been successfully communicated to the client.

The Process of Learning in Therapy

It has been our experience that when these five conditions exist, a process of change inevitably occurs. The client's rigid perceptions of himself and of others loosen and become open to reality. The rigid ways in which he has construed the meaning of his experience are looked at, and he finds himself questioning many of the "facts" of his life, discovering that they are only "facts" because he has regarded them so. He discovers feelings of which he has been unaware, and experiences them, often vividly, in the therapeutic relationship. Thus he learns to be more open to all of his experience -- the evidence within himself as well as the evidence without. He learns to *be* more of his experience -- to be the feelings of which he has been frightened as well as the feelings he has regarded as more acceptable. He becomes a more fluid, changing, learning person.

The Mainspring of Change
In this process it is not necessary for the therapist to "motivate" the client or to supply the energy which brings about the change. Nor, in some sense, is the motivation supplied by the client, at least in any conscious way. Let us say rather that the motivation for learning and change springs from the self-actualizing tendency of life itself, the tendency for the organism to flow into all the differentiated channels of potential development, insofar as these are experienced as enhancing.

I could go on at very considerable length on this, but it is not my purpose to focus on the process of therapy and the learnings which take place, nor on the motivation for these learnings, but rather on the conditions which make them possible. So I will simply conclude this description of therapy by saying that it is a type of significant learning which takes place when five conditions are met:

When the client perceives himself as faced by a serious and meaningful problem;

When the therapist is a congruent person in the relationship, able to *be* the person he *is*;

When the therapist feels an unconditional positive regard for the client;

When the therapist experiences an accurate empathic understanding of the client's private world, and communicates this;

When the client to some degree experiences the therapist's congruence, acceptance, and empathy.

Implications for Education

What do these conditions mean if applied to education? Undoubtedly the teacher will be able to give a better answer than I out of his own experience, but I will at least suggest some of the implications.

Contact with Problems

In the first place it means that significant learning occurs more readily in relation to situations perceived as problems. I believe I have observed evidence to support this. In my own varying attempts to conduct courses and groups in ways consistent with my therapeutic experience, I have found such an approach more effective, I believe, in workshops than in regular courses, in extension courses than in campus courses. Individuals who come to workshops or extension courses are those who are in contact with problems which they recognize as problems. The student in the regular university course, and particularly in the required course, is apt to view the course as an experience in which he expects to remain passive or resentful or both, an experience which he certainly does not often see as relevant to his own problems.

Yet it has also been my experience that when a regular university class does perceive the course as an experience they can use to resolve problems which *are* of concern to them, the sense of release, and the thrust of forward movement is astonishing. And this is true of courses as diverse as Mathematics and Personality.

I believe the current situation in Russian education also supplies evidence on this point. When a whole nation perceives itself as being faced with the urgent problem of being behind -- in agriculture, in industrial production, in scientific development, in weapons development -- then an astonishing amount of significant learning takes place, of which the Sputniks are but one observable example.

So the first implication for education might well be that we permit the student, at any level, to be in real contact with the relevant problems of his existence, so that he perceives problems and issues which he wishes to resolve. I am quite aware that this implication, like the others I shall mention, runs sharply contrary to the current trends in our culture, but I shall comment on that later.

I believe it would be quite clear from my description of therapy that an overall implication for education would be that the task of the teacher is to create a facilitating classroom climate in which significant learning can take place. This general implication can be broken down into several subsections.

The Teacher's Real-ness
Learning will be facilitated, it would seem, if the teacher is congruent. This involves the teachers' being the person that he is, and being openly aware of the attitudes he holds. It means that he feels acceptant toward his own real feelings. Thus he becomes a real person in the relationship with his students. He can be enthusiastic about subjects he likes, and bored by topics he does not like. He can be angry, but he can also be sensitive or sympathetic. Because he accepts his feeling as *his* feelings, he has no need to impose them on his students, or to insist that they feel the same way. He is a *person*, not a faceless embodiment of a curricular requirement, or a sterile pipe through which knowledge is passed from one generation to the next.

I can suggest only one bit of evidence which might support this view. As I think back over a number of teachers who have facilitated my own learning, it seems to me each one has this quality of being a real person. I wonder if your memory is the same. If so, perhaps it is less important that a teacher cover the allotted amount of the curriculum, or use the most approved audio-visual devices, than that he be congruent, real, in his relation to his students.

Acceptance and Understanding

Another implication for the teacher is that significant learning may take place if the teacher can accept the student as he is, and can understand the feelings he possesses. Taking the third and fourth conditions of therapy as specified above, the teacher who can warmly accept, who can provide an unconditional positive regard, and who can empathize with the feelings of fear, anticipation, and discouragement which are involved in meeting new material, will have done a great deal toward wetting the conditions for learning. Clark Moustakas, in his book, *The Teacher and the Child*, has given many excellent examples of individual and group situations from kindergarten to high school, in which the teacher has worked toward just this type of goal. It will perhaps disturb some that when the teacher holds such attitudes, when he is willing to be acceptant of feelings, it is not only attitudes toward school work itself which are expressed, but feelings about parents, feelings of hatred for brother or sister, feelings of concern about self -- the whole gamut of attitudes. Do such feelings have a right to exist openly in a school setting? It is my thesis that they do. They are related to the person's becoming, to his effective learning and effective functioning, and to deal understandingly and acceptantly with such feelings has a definite relationship to the learning of long division or the geography of Pakistan.

Provision of Resources

This brings me to another implication which therapy holds for education. In therapy the resources for learning one's self lie within. There is very little data which the therapist can supply which will be of help since the data to be dealt with exist within the person. In education this is not true. There are many resources of knowledge, of techniques, of theory, which constitute raw material for use. It seems to me that what I have said about therapy suggests that these materials, these resources, be made available to the students, not forced upon them. Here a wide range of ingenuity and sensitivity is an asset.

I do not need to list the usual resources which come to mind -- books, maps, workbooks, materials, recordings, workspace, tools, and the like. Let me focus for a moment on the way the teacher uses himself and his knowledge and experience as a resource. If the teacher holds the point of view I have been expressing then he would probably want to make himself available to his class in at least the following ways:

He would want to let them know of special experience and knowledge he has in the field, and to let them know they could call on his knowledge. Yet he would not want them to feel that they must use him in this way.

He would want them to know that his own way of thinking about the field, and of organizing it, was available to them, even in lecture form, if they wished. Yet again he would want this to be perceived as an offer, which could as readily be refused as accepted.

He would want to make himself known as a resource-finder. Whatever might be seriously wanted by an individual or by the whole group to promote their learning, he would be very willing to consider the possibilities of obtaining such a resource.

He would want the quality of his relationship to the group to be such that his feelings could be freely available to them, without being imposed on them or becoming a restrictive influence on them. He thus could share the excitements and enthusiasms of his own learnings, without insisting that the students follow in his footsteps; the feelings of disinterest, satisfaction, bafflement, or pleasure which he feels toward individual or group activities, without this becoming either a carrot or a stick for the student. His hopes would be that he could say, simply for himself, "I don't like that," and that the student with equal freedom could say, "But I do."

Thus what ever the resource he supplies -- a book, space to work, a new tool, an opportunity for observation of an industrial process, a lecture based on his own study, a picture, graph or map, his own emotional reactions -- he would feel that these were, and would hope they would be perceived as, offerings to be used if they were useful to the student. He would not feel them to be guides, or expectations, or commands, or impositions or requirements. He would offer himself, and all the other resources he could discover, for use.

The Basic Motive

It should be clear from this that his basic reliance would be upon the self-actualizing tendency in his students. The hypothesis upon which he would build is that students who are in real contact with life problems wish to learn, want to grow, seek to find out, hope to master, desire to create. He would see his function as that of developing such a personal relationship with his students, and such a climate in his class room, that these natural tendencies could come to their fruition.

Some Omissions

These I see as some of the things which are implied by a therapeutic viewpoint for the educational process. To make them a bit sharper, let me point out some of the things which are not implied.

I have not included lectures, talks, or expositions of subject matter which are imposed on the students. All of these procedures might be a part of the experience if they were desired, explicitly or implicitly, by the students. Yet even here, a teacher whose work was following through a hypothesis based on therapy would be quick to sense a shift in that desire. He might have been requested to lecture to the group (and to give a *requested* lecture is *very* different from the usual classroom experience), but if he detected a growing disinterest and boredom, he would respond to that, trying to understand the feeling which had arisen in the group, since his response to their feelings and attitudes would take precedence over his interest in expounding material.

I have not included any program of evaluation of the student's learnings in terms of external criteria. I have not, in other words, included examinations. I believe that the testing of the student's achievements in order to see if he meets some criterion held by the teacher, is directly contrary to the implications of therapy for significant learning. In therapy, the examinations are set by *life*. The client meets them, sometimes passing, sometimes failing. He finds that he can use the resources of the therapeutic relationship and his experience in it to organize himself so that he can meet life's tests more satisfyingly next time. I see this as the paradigm for education also. Let me try to spell out a fantasy of what it would mean.

In such an education, the requirements for many life situations would be a part of the resources the teacher provides. The student would have available the knowledge that he cannot enter engineering school without so much math; that he cannot get a job in X corporation unless he has a college diploma; that he cannot become a psychologist without doing an independent doctoral research; that he cannot be a doctor without knowledge of chemistry; that he cannot even drive a car without passing an examination on rules of the road. These are requirements set, not by the teacher, but by life. The teacher is there to provide the resources which the student can use to learn so as to be able to meet these tests.

There would be other in-school evaluations of similar sort. The student might well be faced with the fact that he cannot join the Math Club until he makes a certain score on a standardized mathematics test; that he cannot develop his camera film until he has shown an adequate knowledge of chemistry and lab techniques; that he cannot join the special literature section until he has shown evidence of both wide reading and creative writing. The natural place of evaluation in life is as a ticket of entrance, not as a club over the recalcitrant. Our experience in therapy would suggest that it should be the same way in the school. It would leave the student as a self-respecting, self motivated person, free to choose whether he wished to put forth the effort to gain these tickets of entrance. It would thus refrain from forcing him into conformity, from sacrificing his creativity, and from causing him to live his life in terms of the standards of others.

I am quite aware that the two elements of which I have just been speaking -- the lectures and expositions imposed by the teacher on the group, and the evaluation of the individual by the teacher, constitute the two major ingredients of current education. So when I say that experience in psychotherapy would suggest that they both be omitted, it should be quite clear that the implications of psychotherapy for education are startling indeed.

Probable Outcomes

If we are to consider such drastic changes as I have outlined, what would be the results which would justify them? There have been some research investigations of the outcomes of a student-centered type of teaching, though these studies are far from adequate. For one thing, the situations studied vary greatly in the extent to which they meet the conditions I have described. Most of them have extended only over a period of a few months, though one recent study with lower class children extended over a full year. Some involved the use of adequate controls, some do not.

I think we may say that these studies indicate that in classroom situations which at least attempt to approximate the climate I have described, the findings are as follows: Factual and curricular learning is roughly equal to the learning in conventional classes. Some studies report slightly more, some slightly less. The student-centered group shows gains significantly greater than the conventional class in personal adjustment, in self-initiated extra-curricular learning, in creativity, in self-responsibility.

I have come to realize, as I have considered these studies, and puzzled over the design of better studies which should be more informative and conclusive, that findings from such research will never answer our questions. For all such findings must be evaluated in terms of the goals we have for education. If we value primarily the learning of knowledge, then we may discard the conditions I have described as useless, since there is no evidence that they lead to a greater rate or amount of factual knowledge. We may then favor such measures as the one which I understand is advocated by a number of members of Congress -- the setting up of a training school for scientists, modeled upon the military academies. But if we value creativity, if we deplore the fact that all of our germinal ideas in atomic physics, in psychology, and in other sciences have been borrowed from Europe, then we may wish to give a trial to ways of facilitating learning which give more promise of freeing the mind. If we value independence, if we are disturbed by the growing conformity of knowledge, of values, of attitudes, which our present system induces, then we may wish to set up conditions of learning which make for uniqueness, for self-direction, and for self-initiated learning.

Some Concluding Issues

I have tried to sketch the kind of education which would be implied by what we have learned in the field of psychotherapy. I have endeavored to suggest very briefly what it would mean if the central focus of the teacher's effort were to develop a relationship, an atmosphere, which was conducive to self-motivated, self-actualizing, significant learning. But this is a direction which leads sharply away from current educational practices and educational trends. Let me mention a few of the very diverse issues and questions which need to be faced if we are to think constructively about such an approach.

In the first place, how do we conceive the goals of education? The approach I have outlined has, I believe, advantages for achieving certain goals, but not for achieving others. We need to be clear as to the way we see the purposes of education.

What are the actual outcomes of the kind of education I have described? We need a great deal more of rigorous, hard-headed research to know the actual results of this kind of education as compared with conventional education. Then we can choose on the basis of the facts.

Even if we were to try such an approach to the facilitation of learning, there are many difficult issues. Could we possibly permit students to come in contact with real issues? Our whole culture-- through custom, through the law, through the efforts of labor unions and management, through the attitudes of parents and teachers -- is deeply committed to keeping young people away from any touch with real problems. They are not to work, they should not carry responsibility, they have no business in civic or political problems, they have no place in international concerns, they simply should be guarded from any direct contact with the real problems of individual and group living. They are not expected to help about the home, to earn a living, to contribute to science, to deal with moral issues. This is a deep seated trend which has lasted for more than a generation. Could it possibly be reversed?

Another issue is whether we could permit knowledge to be organized in and by the individual, or whether it is to be organized *for* the individual. Here teachers and educators line up with parents and national leaders to insist that the pupil must be guided. He must be inducted into knowledge we have organized for him. He cannot be trusted to organize knowledge in functional terms for himself. As Herbert Hoover says of high school students, "You simply cannot expect kids of those ages to determine the sort of education they need unless they have some guidance." This seems so obvious to most people that even to question it is to seem somewhat unbalanced. Even a chancellor of a university questions whether freedom is really necessary in education, saying that perhaps we have overestimated its value. He says the Russians have advanced mightily in science without it, and implies that we should learn from them.

Still another issue is whether we would wish to oppose the strong current trend toward education as drill in factual knowledge. All must learn the same facts in the same way. Admiral Rickover states it as his belief that "in some fashion we must devise a way to introduce uniform standards into American education. . . . For the first time, parents would have a real yardstick to measure their schools. If the local school continued to teach such pleasant subjects as 'life adjustment' . . . instead of French and physics, its diploma would be, for all the world to see, inferior." This is a statement of a very prevalent view. Even such a friend of forward-looking views in education as Max Lerner says at one point, "All that a school can ever hope to do is to equip the student with tools which he can later use to become an educated man". It is quite clear that he despairs of significant learning taking place in our school system, and feels that it must take place outside. All the school can do is to pound in the tools.

One of the most painless ways of inculcating such factual tool knowledge is the "teaching machine" being devised by B.F. Skinner and his associates. This group is demonstrating that the teacher is an outmoded and ineffective instrument for teaching arithmetic, trigonometry, French, literary appreciation, geography, or other factual subjects. There is simply no doubt in my mind that these teaching machines, providing immediate rewards for "right" answers, will be further developed, and will come into wide use. Here is a new contribution from the field of the behavioral sciences with which we must come to terms. Does it take the place of the approach I have described, or is it supplemental to it?   He is one of the problems we must consider as we face toward the future.

I hope that by posing these issues, I have made it clear that the double-barreled question of what constitutes significant learning, and how it is to be achieved, poses deep and serious problems for all of us. It is not a time when timid answers will suffice.   I have tried to give a definition of significant learning as it appears in psychotherapy, and a description of the conditions which facilitate such learning.   I have tried to indicate some implications of these conditions for education.   I have, in other words, proposed one answer to these questions.   Perhaps we can use what I have said, against the twin backdrops of current public opinion and current knowledge in the behavioral sciences, as a start for discovering some fresh answers of our own.

DISCUSSION

Rogers makes it very clear in this article that the traditional methods of education are in need of revision. Methods based upon fear of punishment and rote memorization of facts are damaging to the dignity and self-worth of the individual. Experience does seem to indicate that many children (and adults) are resentful when it comes to school and more specifically of learning, which becomes more of a mandated chore rather than a fulfilling positive experience.

Rogers further asserts that characteristics of the teacher can be of paramount importance in the successful schooling of the student. Much like the psychotherapist, the learner is best served by a teacher who is knowledgeable, caring, non-judgmental, and able to fully accept each and every student as unique and special individuals.

Rogers' ideas are not completely original. We have seen and will encounter other thinkers who have voiced criticism at the traditional punitive methods (Locke, Rousseau, Skinner), and have suggested self-discovery as a viable method for learning (Confucius, Rousseau, Piaget). However, Rogers must be given credit for linking the positive changes that occur during therapy, including growth, increased self-esteem, and insight into oneself with similar desirable outcomes in the student. Since the end results for these two populations are very much alike, why not use methods which have been shown to be effective in producing these results? No one would deny that Rogers has identified some very positive attributes of students; perhaps accepting his suggestion would indeed help to bring them into reality.

Discussion   Questions

1.   Rogers lists several characteristics that teachers should ideally possess.   What are these characteristics?   Further, how would an aspiring teacher go about getting these qualities in the first place?   What implications for teacher education do you see?

2.   If grades were in fact abolished, what type of feedback could be given to students?   Would the teacher be able to clearly discern between students and their abilities?   If so, how?

3.   At what level should Rogers' system be implemented?   Do you think that students in college would be able to adjust and accept this system when they had completed their previous learning in a more traditional manner?

4.   Would it be possible to modify Rogers ideas so that they could be incorporated into a more traditional approach to education?   Which ones would you include?

CHAPTER THIRTEEN

B. F. SKINNER

If you were to call B. F. Skinner a practical man, he probably would have smiled and said "Thank you; the successful application of theoretical principles has always been most important to me." For most of his long and productive life, Burris Frederic Skinner, working in his laboratory with his rats and his pigeons, has carefully and repeatedly demonstrated that the principles of operant conditioning can be accomplished with highly predictable results. The connection between what a person (or animal) does and the effect they produce on their environment has emerged from the carefully controlled experimental manipulations of the lab and into the classroom for the betterment (and, unfortunately, sometimes the detriment) of the student. Before we look into the details of operant learning, let us first examine the life of Skinner.

The elder of two sons, Burris Frederick Skinner (Fred to his friends) was born on March 20, 1904 in Susquehanna, Pennsylvania. At an early age he showed a fondness and fascination for animals, and had numerous "pets" (including birds, lizards, mice and turtles) that he would carefully study. He was also quite skilled at the construction of various gadgets and original equipment (such as a steam cannon that could be used to shoot potatoes at unsuspecting victims). His mother and father were loving, but strict in their convictions that the most important aspect in living is what one does (that is, how one behaves, and not necessarily how one thinks). As a lawyer, his father made numerous attempts to impress upon his son the merits of proper conduct, and the punishments given to those who disobey the law. His interest in the behavior of animals, his knack for building various sorts of apparatus, and an ingraining of the importance of the behavior of an individual would lead the way for his eventual life's work as the best known psychologist of the 20th century.

Skinner attended Hamilton College in New York, majoring in English and hoping to become a writer. Although his stories were highly endorsed by the great poet Robert Frost, Skinner became discouraged with writing and, after reading John Watson's Behaviorism, applied to Harvard to pursue graduate work in experimental psychology. Not satisfied with the emphasis on the structure of consciousness, and convinced that behavior was more complicated than an understanding of the conditioned responses of Watson, Skinner began his carefully controlled studies of the behavior of animals in order to gain a theoretical understanding of the laws governing behavior. The fully developed model, which is called Operant Conditioning, was formulated by Skinner over the next sixty years. Although initially convinced that operant learning could be used as a model for a utopian society (upon which he elaborated in his best seller, Walden II), he realized years later that the governing of an entire society was probably too ambitious a project, and settled for more limited uses of operant learning. Throughout his long and productive life, Skinner was a dogmatic force in the usefulness of operant learning techniques, and a strong opponent of "mentalistic" viewpoints within psychology. His methods have proven successful in the modification of behavior of mentally ill patients, retarded individuals, prisoners, workers in industrial settings, and students of all ages and backgrounds. As it is necessary to understand his system before we can appreciate its application, we now turn to a general discussion of operant learning. We will then see how its principles can be incorporated into the classroom.

In almost all situations the occurrence of a behavior is followed (often immediately) by a consequence within the environment. A baby shakes a rattle, and a noise is produced.

A student raises her hand, and the teacher pays attention to her. It is clear that some behaviors are followed by pleasant or desirable results, while other behaviors produce pain, embarrassment, or other unfortunate consequences. While exceptions to the rule exist, most people would agree that we strive to maximize our positive consequences by engaging in behaviors which will bring them about, and conversely attempt to minimize those behaviors which cause us to be uncomfortable. We might then state that behaviors which bring about beneficial results will become strengthened and are likely to be repeated in similar settings, while behaviors which result in some sort of discomfort to the individual will become weakened and eventually replaced with other more adaptable behaviors.

Skinner went on to demonstrate that behaviors could be strengthened in two ways: by removing an unpleasant effect (negative reinforcement), or be producing a desirable effect (positive reinforcement). Notice that in both instances, the behavior is first displayed, and only then is some sort of consequence established. For example, a student might learn that by completing his homework, he is allowed to play outside. The student might also learn that praise and compliments from the teacher will be the result of a well prepared homework assignment. In this case, the teacher has used positive reinforcement to strengthen the desired behavior.

While positive and negative reinforcement serve to increase the chances of a behavior being repeated, punishment and extinction have the opposite effect; they both will cause a decrease in the likelihood of the behavior being shown in the future. Punishment involves the application of painful or in some other way aversive consequence after the appearance of a behavior. For example, it was not so many years ago that teachers were allowed to spank their students for certain acts. The pain and public embarrassment of the spanking was thought to be sufficient to eliminate those behaviors but, as Skinner points out, this oversimplifies the problem of inappropriate behavior, and leaves unfortunate side effects upon the student. (Skinner has never advocated the use of punishment for the removal of a behavior). As an alternative to punishment, behavior may be eliminated by removing privileges or other fun and desirable activities for misbehavior. Extinction, as Skinner calls this process, is widely used today. The student who must sit in the corner, or who in some way is prevented from enjoying the activities of the classroom will learn to remove the behavior in question, and to replace it with more acceptable forms of interaction. The latter, of course, will be strengthened by positive reinforcement.

We have seen that behavior can be both strengthened or weakened by the application of the above principles. It is also possible to modify behavior with the introduction of schedules of reinforcement. Skinner and his colleagues spent years outlining the effects of different methods of delivering reinforcement to their subjects. The simplest schedule, called a continuous schedule of reinforcement, involves providing feedback after each response or behavior. A teacher might call on a student every time she raises her hand, and ignore her each time she volunteers an answer without first raising her had. In the first case, she is using continuous positive reinforcement, while in the second example she is employing the method of continuous extinction. Continuous schedules are especially useful when the individual is learning a behavior for the first time; the constant feedback gives them confidence that whatever they are doing is correct, or conversely, that other behaviors will always be met with either punishment or extinction.

However, once a behavior has been acquired, a partial or intermittent schedule will often suffice. Under this strategy, behaviors are only occasionally reinforced. As an example, suppose a teacher wants to encourage perfect attendance. It might be impractical to reinforce the entire class for every session of perfect attendance, but an occasional special treat for all students (such as a field trip) will motivate the students to want to come to school. The key factor in this case is the unpredictability of the reward; from the students point of view, they are never certain when the desired field trip will occur. This unpredictable outcome tends to keep the level of response high.

It is also possible to use partial schedules on a very predictable basis. The teacher might tell the class that after ten consecutive sessions of perfect attendance, they will go on a field trip. In this instance all students are aware of the nearness of the goal, and all will be motivated to bring it about. This particular schedule is called a fixed ratio schedule, in that the number of responses relative to the reward is constant (ten perfect attendances equals one field trip).

The concepts of reinforcement and schedules of reinforcement constitute the essential aspects of Skinner's theory of operant learning. We have already seen several examples of how these principles might operate from the perspective of both the teacher and the student. Before moving on to the Skinner reading, it might be helpful to consider one more example utilizing several of the above ideas.

Most students today are familiar with the use of computers to aid in the teaching and learning of school subjects. Computers offer several advantages, and in fact Skinner was one of the earliest proponents of teaching machines in the classroom. To begin with, the machines are rewarding in and of themselves; that is, they are fun to use. A teacher might then be able to offer the use of the computer as a positive reinforcement for several of her students. The computer operates on a continuous schedule of reinforcements for the student. The pupil knows if their answer is correct or not right after it is given. Immediate feedback has been shown to be most effective in the learning of skills and ideas. Should the answer provided be incorrect, the program will trace the probable source of the error and branch to another portion of the program intended to strengthen the students behavior in this regard. Then, with the use of small increments, the skill or idea will be represented to the student until mastery has occurred (a process Skinner refers to a shaping). As an added benefit, each student can proceed at their own individual pace; some faster, some slower, but all at a speed that is best for them (and, when you consider the common plight of the classroom teacher concerning the speed of presentation of material, this is a tremendous advantage). At the end of a particular lesson, the computer can generate a small number of quiz questions over the material, with perhaps a score of 90 or above to signify that the student has mastered the concept. The quiz could then be printed out and shown to the teacher and parents for additional positive praise and reinforcement.

Notice the difference between this scenario and the more traditional "learn this or else" approach that the student often faces. The latter is punitive and often carries with it fear, intimidation, and a general resentment of school. While not all lessons (nor school finances) are best suited for computer instruction, the general concepts can be employed in the more traditional framework of teaching.

The following article by Skinner was first published in 1969. By this time most of the particulars of operant learning had been formulated in the lab, and were ready to be utilized in the real world. The classroom provides an ideal setting for the conscientious teacher to use reinforcement, scheduling and shaping techniques to make the school experience a challenging and rewarding environment for the student. Notice how in the reading Skinner is arguing against the general idea that all that is necessary for successful education is to change the "attitude" of the students towards school; what one must do instead is to reinforce proper and successful behaviors, which will in turn modify the student's outlook and perceptions.

SKINNER ON CONTINGENCY MANAGEMENT IN THE CLASSROOM*

Why do students go to school? Why do they behave themselves in class? Why do they study and learn and remember? These are important questions, but they are seldom asked--possibly because we are not proud of the answers. Whether we like it or not, most students still come to school, behave themselves, and study in order to avoid the consequences of not doing so. True, most teachers have abandoned the birch rod (though its return is called for in some quarters), but there are many ingenious, less violent replacements. Violent or not, punitive methods have serious consequences, among them truancy, apathy, resentment, vandalism and ultimately an anti-intellectualism which includes an unwillingness to support education. These are the great problems of the educational establishment, and they can be traced in large part to the techniques of the establishment itself.

Few teachers are happy about punitive methods (most of them would like to be friends with their students), but alternatives have seldom proved fruitful. Simply to abandon punishment and allow students to do as they please is to abandon the goals of education. A "free school" was recently described in a newspaper article as follows:

The middle school classroom I saw was full of children working in an endless variety of subjects, the life cycle of the beetle, action painting, physical properties of water, mathematics (by choice), making dressing-up clothes, writing poetry. Some of them wandered up and started a conversation. They were confident and articulate. I was asked to join various

* **Source**: B. F. Skinner, from **Education**, 1969. Reprinted by permission of the author.

games, give an honest opinion on a painting, listen to poetry. Ten year old Michael is writing poetry nearly all the time now....Another child is coaxing a woodworm out of the piece of rotting wood.

It is no doubt an attractive picture--until we start to think about what a school is for.

Men have been dreaming of the permissive or free school for at least two hundred years. The idea first appeared in close association with the idea of political freedom, and one man-- Jean Jacques Rousseau--was largely responsible for both. He has been credited with inspiring not only the French Revolution but, in his great work *Emile*, a revolution of perhaps comparable magnitude in education. He was interested quite justly, in abolishing the punitive methods of his time, and so were the disciples who followed him--Pestalozzi, Froebel and his kindergarten, Montessori, John Dewey, and (ad absurdum) Neill with his Summerhill.

With Rousseau the proposal was clearly a dream, for Emile was an imaginary student with, as we now know, imaginary learning processes. When Pestalozzi tried Rousseau's principles on his own child, he came to grief. And, sooner or later, the dream is almost always followed by a rude awakening. Secondary schools are founded by well-intentioned people who want their students to be free, but the schools grow steadily more disciplined as the exigencies of teaching make themselves felt. When prospective parents begin to ask "How many of your students go on to college?" and "What colleges do they go to?" the goal of the free student is abandoned. Courses show the same pattern. Language instruction begins painlessly with the direct method, but sooner or later the student will be found memorizing vocabulary lists and grammatical paradigms. And one of the freedoms enjoyed by the students in Summerhill was the freedom to treat their fellows punitively.

Occasionally the dream comes true. In any generation there are a few outstanding teachers, just as there are a few outstanding artists, writers, executives, and personalities in films and television. There are also many exceptional students--students who scarcely need to be taught at all. An outstanding teacher and a few good students compose a picture that we should all like to copy, but it is not a model for the teaching of ordinary students by ordinary teachers.

Nor can we replace punishment simply by telling our students about long-term advantages. We make a great deal of the "dollar value" of an education (conveniently overlooking the fact that truck drivers and carpenters make as much as most teachers), but the ultimate consequences of an education are too remote to have any important effect on the student as he reads or listens to a lecture. The gold stars, marks, grades, honors, promotion, and prizes which we think of as alternatives to punitive sanctions also lack a necessary immediacy. Nor can we solve the problem by bringing real life into the classroom so that students will come into contact with things which are naturally rewarding, for we cannot find interesting things relevant to everything we want to teach. "Real life" philosophies of education have also meant the abandonment of important goals.

All these measures fail because they do not give the student adequate reasons for studying and learning. Punishment gave him a reason (we can say that for it), but if we are to avoid unwanted by-products, we must find nonpunitive forms. It is not an impossible assignment. The "reasons" why men behave are to be found among the consequences of their behavior--what, to put it roughly, they "get out of behaving in given ways." And these have been carefully studied. Behavior which acts upon the environment to produce consequences--"operant" behavior--has been experimentally analyzed in great detail. Certain kinds of consequences called reinforcers (among them the things the layman calls rewards) are made contingent upon what an organism is doing and upon the circumstances under which it is doing it. Changes in behavior are then observed.

The contingencies, rather that the reinforcers, are the important things. It has long been obvious that men act to achieve pleasure and avoid pain (at least most of the time), but the fact to be emphasized is what they are doing at the moment they achieve these results. Special equipment is used to arrange so-called "contingencies of reinforcement" (and if teaching can be defined as the expediting of learning, then this equipment is a kind of teaching machine). The complexity of the equipment to be found in hundreds of laboratories throughout the world is not a bad indicator of the complexity of the contingencies now under investigation. Few people outside the field are aware of how far the analysis has gone. As more and more complex contingencies have been arranged, it has been possible to study more and more complex kinds of behavior, including behavior once attributed to higher mental processes.

An application to education was inevitable, but it has not been unopposed. The fact that much of the early work involved the behavior of lower animals such as rats and pigeons has often been held against it. But man is an animal, although an extraordinarily complex one, and shares many basic behavioral processes with other species. Human behavior must nevertheless be studied in its own right, and human subjects are in fact now commonly used in experimental analyses. When comparable contingencies of reinforcement can be arranged, they yield comparable results; but the contingencies to which the human organism can adjust are extraordinarily complex. Efforts currently under analysis have the subtlety, variety, and intricacy which characterize human behavior in the world at large.

That the methods of an experimental analysis of operant behavior are appropriate to human subjects is confirmed by the success with which they have been put to work in practical ways. Psychotherapy, for example, has undergone an important change. A recent book by Ayllon and Azrin, *The Token Economy*, shows how a hospital for psychotics can be converted into a community in which patients care for themselves and their possessions, avoid trouble with their associates and (within the limits imposed by their illness) enjoy life. Such an arrangement of contingencies of reinforcement has been called a "prosthetic" environment. Like eye glasses, hearing aids, and artificial limbs, it permits people to behave successfully in spite of defects. In the psychotic the defect is often an insensitivity to contingencies of reinforcements.

The principles of operant conditioning were first applied to education in programmed instruction. The step-by-step shaping of complex behavior was first demonstrated in an experimental analysis, and the technique is probably still best seen in experiments with animals. A hungry pigeon, for example, can be induced through reinforcement with food to respond in specified ways. Quite complex forms of behavior can be generated, often with surprising speed, through a series of stages leading to the terminal specifications. One actually "sees learning take place," and the visibility is important. When a teacher can bring about conspicuous changes in behavior, changes which do not need to be confirmed by a statistical treatment of test scores, he knows immediately what he has done, and he is then most likely to learn to teach effectively. Traditional research in learning has seldom been very useful in education, and in part because it has neglected the process of shaping. Subjects have been plunged into terminal contingencies and left to struggle toward adequate forms of behavior through "trial and error." (Although shaping is important, it is not always necessary. There are effective ways of evoking complex behavior so that it can be directly reinforced, and there is often a great gain in efficiency. Relevant techniques can also be attributed to the experimental analysis of behavior.)

Programmed instruction has been largely responsible for the current emphasis on behavioral specifications.   A program can be written only when certain basic questions have been answered.   What is the student to do as the result of having been taught?   To say that a program is to "impart knowledge," "train rational powers," or "make students creative" is not to identify the changes which are actually to be brought about. Something more specific is needed to design effective programmed contingencies (as it is needed in order to teach well in the classroom).   We do not teach the skills students are said to display when they behave skillfully, we teach skillful behavior.   We do not impart knowledge, we generate behavior said to show the possession of knowledge.   We do not improve abilities or strengthen rational powers; we make it more likely that the student will show the behavior from which abilities and powers are inferred.   When goals are properly specified, the teacher knows what he is to do and, later, whether he has done it.   Behavioral objectives remove much of the mystery from education, and teachers may feel demeaned when their task is reduced to less awesome dimensions.   But the loss is more than offset by a greater sense of achievement.

Many early programs were constructed by writers who missed some of the implications of the basic analysis.   They were encouraged to do so by educational philosophers who tried to assimilate programming to traditional theories of learning.   Programming was said to be simply a matter of proceeding in small steps, of asking the student to master one step before moving on to the next, of arranging steps in a logical sequence with no gaps, and so on.   This was true enough, and programs designed on these principles were better than no programs at all, but other points need to be considered.   An important example has to do with "motivation."

Studies of operant reinforcement differ from earlier studies of learning by emphasizing the maintenance as well as the acquisition of behavior.   Acquisition is the conspicuous change brought about by reinforcement, but the maintenance of behavior in a given state of strength is an equally important effect. A good program reinforces the student abundantly and at just the right times. It shapes new forms of behavior under the control of appropriate stimuli, but the important thing is that it maintains the student's behavior. It holds his attention; it keeps him at work.

Traditional studies of learning have paid little attention to why the student learns, and this has encouraged the belief that men have a natural curiosity or love of learning, or that they naturally want to learn. We do not say that about a pigeon; we say only that under the conditions we have arranged, a pigeon learns. We should say the same thing about human students. Given the right conditions men will learn-- not because they want to, but because, as the result of the genetic endowment of the species, contingencies bring about changes in behavior. One of the main differences between a textbook and a program is that a textbook teaches only when students have been given some extraneous reason for studying it. A program contains its own reasons. Fortunately for us all, the human organism is reinforced by many things. Success is one of them. A baby shakes a rattle because the production of noise is reinforcing, and adults put jigsaw puzzles together and work crossword puzzles for no more obvious reason than that they come out right. In a good program the student makes things come out right; he makes things work; he brings order out of chaos. A good program helps him do so. It makes right responses highly probable- just short of telling him what they are. Again the motivational issue may be missed. Many people resist making a student's task easy, and the beginning programmer may find himself unwilling to "give a response away." As a teacher he has felt the need to keep students under aversive control, and he may not yet be fully aware of his power to control them in other ways.

A program is also reinforcing because it clarifies progress. It has a definite size. The student knows when he is half-way through and when he has finished. Because of all this a good program pulls the student forward. He may feel exhausted when he has finished, but he does not need to force himself to work.

There is another problem in education which operant reinforcement helps to solve. In primary and secondary schools (and to some extent at other levels) a teacher not only teaches, he has custody of his students for an appreciable part of the day. Their behavior in the classroom, quite apart from what they are learning, is part of his assignment. Coming to class, behaving well toward other students, attending to the teacher, entering into discussions, studying--these are as essential to education as what is being learned, and here the teacher plays a different role. He is not a source of knowledge or an evaluator of what a student knows; he is in a sense the governor of a community.

It should be a community in which learning takes place expeditiously, and the teacher can meet that assignment if he knows how to use reinforcement. But he must first answer an important question: what reinforcers are available? To put it roughly, what does he possess that his students want? It is often an embarrassing question, but almost never wholly unanswerable. The built-in reinforcers of programmed materials will not suffice, but other things are available.

The physical aspect of a school may or may not be reinforcing, and this will have a bearing on what happens when a student turns a corner and comes in sight of the school. If the building is not attractive, he will be less likely to turn that corner again and may go in some other direction. The appearance of a building is usually beyond the teacher's control, but reinforcing features of a classroom may not be. Business enterprises understand the principle. A well-run store smells good; it is tastefully decorated and pleasantly lighted; there may be music in the background. The behavior of entering the store is therefore reinforced, and customers are more likely to enter it again. To "reduce absenteeism" the teacher should take similar steps to make sure that his students are reinforced when they enter his classroom.

What goes on in the room is also relevant. The aversive techniques of the birch rod or cane are not likely to reinforce coming to school, and students so treated are likely to play truant or become drop-outs when they can legally do so. Social contingencies are important. A child is more likely to come to school if he gets along with his peers and his teacher; he is not likely to come if he is frequently criticized, attacked, or ostracized.

Unfortunately, social contingencies are often hard to arrange. To induce the members of a classroom community to behave well with respect to each other, additional reinforcers may be needed. The teacher may have some control over what food children eat at lunchtime, what supplies they are permitted to use, what privileges they can enjoy (such as access to play areas), whom they may associate with, when they may turn to preferred activities, and what field trips they may take. Personal commendation is often a powerful reinforcer, but a merely synthetic approval or affection has its dangers.

The main problem is to make these reinforcers contingent on the desired behavior. They are often not available on the spur of the moment. The teacher cannot conveniently reinforce a child when he sits quietly by sending him off on a field trip, or when he stops fighting by handing him an ice cream cone. A "generalized reinforcer" is needed--something which is exchangeable for reinforcing things. Money shows the archetypal pattern. We pay people even though at the time they receive our money they are not hungry for the food they will buy with it or in the mood for the film they will use it to go to see. Credit points or tokens can be used as money in the classroom. They are relatively independent of the deprivations which make them reinforcing and of the circumstances under which the things they are exchanged for will be consumed.

In one procedure the behavior of the students is sampled from time to time. A student is chosen with some mechanical system such as spinning a dial or drawing a name from a bowl, and his behavior is sampled for, say, 20 or 30 seconds. He is then told that he has been observed and that he has or has not received a token or credit. A day or two of this is often enough to make a great change: the room grows quiet as the students go to work. Sampling can then become less frequent. Eventually, as the students begin to be reinforced in other ways when they find themselves working more effectively in a quiet room, they will construct their own social contingencies, which may eventually replace those arranged by the teacher.

No one procedure will work well in every classroom, and a certain ingenuity is needed to devise the right system in the right place, but the principle of contingency management is sound and it is proving effective in a rapidly increasing number of experiments. Research conducted in a classroom is not always impressive "statistically," but enough has been done to warrant further experimentation on a broad scale.

There are objections, however, and some of them call for comment. Reinforcement is sometimes called bribery. (To say this is to make a confession: a bribe is paid to induce a person to do something he is for some reason inclined not to do, and it is tragic that we are so ready to see school work in that light.) The point of a bribe is an implied contract ("Do this and I will give you that"), but a contract tends to destroy the effect of a reinforcer. Contingencies of reinforcement are most effective when there is no prior agreement as to terms.

A more valid objection is that contingencies of this sort are artificial. In real life one does not sit quietly in order to take a field trip to the zoo or stop annoying one's neighbor in order to get an ice cream cone. The connection between the behavior and its consequence is contrived. (It is curious that no one raises the same objection with respect to punishment, for there is no natural connection between solving a problem in arithmetic and avoiding the cane. And good marks, promotion, honors, and prizes are not only artificial reinforcers, they are artificially and ineffectively contingent on behavior.) But artificiality is not the issue. We use contrived contingencies to set up behavior which will, we hope, be reinforced naturally under the contingencies of daily life. The problem is to make sure that the behavior we set up will indeed be effective in the world at large.

There have often been great discrepancies between what is taught and what students eventually use. Verbal materials are easily imported into the classroom (in the form of discussions, lectures, and textbooks), and they have often been overemphasized. Students spend a great deal of time answering questions, but answering questions is only a small part of daily life. Nonverbal behavior also needs to be taught. But this does not mean that we should get rid of verbal teaching altogether. The value of verbal programs in such a field as medical school anatomy may well be questioned. Nothing but a cadaver will teach the would-be doctor what the human body is like or permit him to acquire the special behaviors he needs.

One would certainly not want to be operated upon by a surgeon who had merely worked through a programmed text in human anatomy. But there is a great deal to be said for programmed instruction before turning to a cadaver. What one learns in verbal or pictorial form facilitates learning about things themselves. There is nothing unreal about verbal material.

Another objection is that reinforcers in daily life are not always immediate, and that the student must be prepared to behave for the sake of remote consequences. No one is ever actually reinforced by remote consequences, but rather by mediating reinforcers which have acquired their power through some connection with them. Mediating reinforcers can be set up, however, and the student can be taught with available principles and techniques to find or construct them for himself.

A rather similar objection is that in daily life a student is not always reinforced when he behaves, and that he should become accustomed to nonreinforcement. But this is a subject which has been studied with particular care. High levels of activity can be sustained by intermittent reinforcement, particularly if the schedule of reinforcement has been suitably programmed. A gambler is reinforced on what is called a "variable-ratio schedule." It may sustain his behavior to the point at which he loses all his money, but it will not have this effect unless the mean ratio of responses to reinforcements has been extended gradually. Students reinforced on a variable-ratio schedule will show a fantastic dedication if the schedule has been properly programmed. They will work for long periods of time with no reinforcement whatsoever, and are thus well prepared for a world in which reinforcements may indeed be rare.

Current applications of operant conditioning to education are no doubt crude, but they are a beginning, and a beginning must be made. The task is particularly difficult because we must contend with theories and practices which are deeply entrenched. There is nothing very new in prevailing educational theories, and it will be a long time before we can properly estimate the harm they have done. Most teachers today teach essentially as teachers have taught for centuries. The best of them are simply people who have a knack in getting along with others. All this must change, and the change will take time. But we are on the verge of a new educational "method"--a new pedagogy--in which the teacher will emerge as a skilled behavioral engineer. He will be able to analyze the contingencies which arise in his classes, and design and set up improved versions. He will know what is to be done and will have the satisfaction of knowing that he has done it.

The training of a teacher should begin with basic principles. Everyone who intends to be a teacher should have a chance to see learning take place or, better, to produce visible learning himself, as by shaping the behavior of a rat or a pigeon. It is a heartening experience to discover that one can produce behavior of specified topography and bring it under the control of specified stimuli. Some such experience is particularly valuable because the effects of positive reinforcement are somewhat delayed in contrast with punishment, which tends to be used in part just because the results are quick. Laboratory or classroom practice in operant conditioning gives the teacher the confidence he needs to change behavior in less immediate but more effective ways.

It also clarifies the mistakes teachers make when they are careless about reinforcement. Many problems in classroom management arise because the teacher reinforces students when they behave in objectionable ways. For example, the teacher may pay special attention when the student uses obscenities or moves about or talks at inappropriate times. The teacher tends to do so "naturally," and he will be dissuaded from doing so only when the effects of reinforcement have been made clear to him.

An example of the misuse of operant reinforcement in the classroom has been analyzed elsewhere. No matter how bad a teacher may be, he has at least one available reinforcer-dismissing his class. If, near the end of a period, he is free to tell his students that they may leave (if there is no routine signal such as a bell), he can use dismissal as a powerful reinforcer. He should wait until the behavior of the class is as acceptable as it is likely to be and then dismiss. But almost inevitably he will do the wrong thing: he will tend to dismiss the class when trouble is brewing. A surreptitious fight is starting in the back of the room and so he says "That's enough for today." In doing so he gets out of today's trouble, but a fight will be more likely to start tomorrow.

Another natural mistake is to shift to a more interesting topic when a discussion or lecture appears to be boring the listener.   A more interesting topic is a reinforcer, and by shifting it we reinforce expressions of boredom.   Another common mistake is to distract the attention of a likely troublemaker.   A distraction is by definition reinforcing, and it reinforces what the student is doing when we distract him--namely, making trouble.   We make mistakes of this sort until a greater familiarity with the principles of reinforcement induces us to stop.

In England a "black paper" recently criticized the educational establishment.   It performed a service by bringing into the open a growing dissatisfaction with current methods. We have been too ready to assume that the student is a free agent, that he wants to learn, that he knows best what he should learn, that his attitudes and tastes should determine what he learns, and that he should discover things for himself rather than learn what others have already discovered.   These principles are all wrong, and they are responsible for much of our current trouble.   Education is primarily concerned with the transmission of a culture--with teaching new members what others have already learned--and it is dangerous to ignore this function.   But the black paper took the wrong line by suggesting that we return to what are essentially punitive techniques.   The teacher must regain control, but he must do so in ways which are not only more efficient but free of the undesirable by-products of older practices.   Progressive education made an honest effort to dispense with punishment, but it never found the alternatives it needed.   Effective alternatives are now available.

The classroom is a kind of community, with a culture of its own, and we can design such a culture while respecting the standards of dignity and freedom which we value in the world at large.   The assignment is important because in the long run education must take its place as the method of choice in all forms of social control.   It must replace the aversive sanctions of government, both international and domestic, and the unduly compelling economic sanctions of business and industry. The by-products are all too visible today, in part because of the violence with which they are attacked. The sooner we find effective means of social control, the sooner we shall produce a culture in which man's potential is fully realized. Those who are genuinely trying to improve education have, therefore, a frightening responsibility, but they face a tremendous opportunity.

DISCUSSION

True to his behavioral orientation, Skinner disavows the notion that "attitude change" within a student will bring about any meaningful behavioral change. Proper motivation does not come from within, rather it is the reinforcing opportunities of the environment that serve to strengthen or reduce behaviors. In Skinner's conception, the teacher is something of a behavioral engineer, one whose skills can create an environment where appropriate reinforcers exist to facilitate learning.

It should also be obvious that punishment is at best a poor technique in correcting problem behaviors. In addition to failing to teach the student anything, it carries the risk that the student will generalize aversive behaviors and feelings towards any and all aspects related to school. School and learning will then become things to avoid rather than things to embrace.

The concept of computer programmed instruction has continued to be an effective and enjoyable method to motivate and reinforce students for learning. Programs now exist which can teach anything from the alphabet to physics. Immediate reinforcement and personal attention are now truly possible with this technology, one which Skinner helped to pioneer.

While most teachers do, either by accident or common sense, utilize methods of Behavioral Psychology, Skinner's work continues to challenge us to analyze our classrooms, identify the contingencies of reinforcement, specify exactly what behaviors we want our students to have, and offer new and varied forms of reinforcement. While not all thinkers adhere as rigidly to this position as he does, few would disagree that it has made a significant contribution to educational theory.

Discussion   Questions

1.   Skinner states that punitive methods will have serious adverse consequences on the student.   What is your orientation towards punishment in the classroom?   If you do use punitive methods in your class, how will you counter the negative effects that Skinner cautions against?

2.   In the reading, Skinner argues for the method of shaping (of complex behavior) over the traditional trial and error method of learning.   Can you envision how the method of shaping might be utilized in your classroom?

3.   A teacher in your school tells you that her main job is to instill self confidence and a positive mental attitude towards learning in her students.   From a Skinnerian point of view, how might you respond to this?

4.   Name four common objections to contingency management in the classroom.   How does Skinner respond to these criticisms?

5.   A teacher notices several students yawning and fiddling with their pencils.   Since there were only ten minutes left in the class period, he decides to dismiss the class early.   Analyze this situation from a behavioral point of view.   What recommendations could you make to this teacher?

CHAPTER FOURTEEN

SHINICHI SUZUKI

Shinichi Suzuki was born in Nagoya, Japan in 1898. His father, Masakichi Suzuki, founded what came to be the single largest violin factory throughout the world. Masakichi was a teacher of English as a second language in Tokyo earlier in his career. Quite by accident he became interested in the manufacturing of violins, and made his first violin in 1888, ten years before Shinichi was born. He began a small factory which was to gradually increase in size. Shinichi was certainly very highly influenced by this and remembers working long hours in his father's factory, and some of the experiences he was to have there went on to influence his life in a major way. Little did Masakichi realize that his son would become recognized throughout the world as a leading teacher of music. The family factory fell on hard times during the depression of the twenties. But more than economic success was already achieved by the Suzuki's. Shinichi saw his father as a man of great character who taught him many moral lessons that he would carry with him the rest of his life. In particular, he credits his father with teaching him "non-materialistic values" as well as "sociability and an eagerness to learn from others." Above all, says Suzuki, it was his father's "smiling face" that he would keep with him forever. No doubt, Suzuki's later emphasis on the importance of good parenting skills, was highly influenced by his own experiences with his father.

Suzuki studied in Tokyo, but admits to being a somewhat reluctant student. He was never "good" as a student, in the sense of receiving good grades. He did, however, excel in leadership and in many instances proved to be of outstanding character (something, again, he may have learned from his father as a young boy). Suzuki went on to study the violin in Germany under the great master Karl Klinger. Of Klinger, Suzuki was to later say in his *Nurtured By Love: A New Approach to Education*, that he "taught me the real essence of music." Klinger was also a man of high character who exhibited courage against the Nazi regime, in particular Klinger openly opposed the attempt by Hitler to denigrate the contribution that Jewish artists and composers had made to the overall artistic genius of Germany. After eight years, Suzuki returned to Japan with his wife Waltrud. He began to teach and also formed a quartet with three of his brothers. His experiences both as a player and as a teacher, especially of the very young students who came to him to learn music, slowly developed into a method which is today recognized worldwide. Suzuki's method, known as "Talent Education", has been developed and utilized internationally. He and his students have given concerts for the United Nations, at the Julliard School of Music, and on many campuses in many nations. *The New York Times* once pronounced that "The most influential teacher of our era is likely to be Dr. Shinichi Suzuki of Japan." And his methods have been so attractive in the United States that it has been referred to as a "Suzuki Explosion."

Throughout his experiences, Suzuki never failed to "learn from others." His world-wide recognition brought him into contact with many great persons, among them the great Pablo Cassals and Albert Einstein. Einstein was a distinctive influence. Suzuki met and became a close friend of Einstein's while in Germany. Einstein was himself an acknowledged virtuoso on the violin and was very impressed with Suzuki. Suzuki tells us that he "learned how to be giving from Einstein." And in their many discussions together, Suzuki relates that Einstein credits his own musical perception as the source for his theory of relativity. Here Einstein may have laid the seed for Suzuki's later conviction that education in music is not just education in music--it is education period.

In considering Suzuki's method of education, or what can be called his philosophy of education, several key ideas emerge as central. Among the first of these is Suzuki's view about talent or ability. The assumption of "talent education" is that "talent is no accident of birth." Countless times Suzuki relates the story most parents who came to him with their children were telling: "does my child have talent?" they would often ask, or "how much talent does my child have?" or even worse, "my child just is not talented, is he?" Suzuki believed that the assumption behind this kind of attitude is erroneous. Talent, he taught, is not something you either have or do not have. It is not a matter of fate, it is "no accident of birth" as he says in *Nurtured By Love.* Suzuki was firmly convinced that the talent or ability that any particular child displays or develops, is greatly dependent on the environment, rather than on inborn traits or the lack thereof. In the same book Suzuki argues that everyone is born with natural abilities, but it is often the "environment that stunts and damages them, and it is assumed that they are born that way . . . . But they are all wrong." And this, he believed, was not only true of music ability or inability, but is a principle he carried over into education as a whole. He goes on to say of those children that teachers have labeled "slow-learners" that "In my opinion the child is not below average in intelligence; it is the educational system that is wrong. His ability or talent was not developed properly." And again, "People are what they are as a result of their own specific environment." It is therefore very frustrating to Suzuki that so many look for solutions in the wrong places. In one his most telling pages of *Nurtured By Love* he writes: "People today are like gardeners who look sadly at ruined saplings and shake their heads, saying these seeds must have been bad to start with, not realizing that the seed was all right, and that it was their method of cultivation that was wrong. They go on in their mistaken way, ruining plant after plant. It is imperative that the human race escape from this vicious circle. The sooner people realize their mistake, the better. The more the situation is changed, the nearer the human race will come to happiness."

Another of Suzuki's convictions was that ability follows character. A motto that he learned as a young man was to become "The principle written on my heart--Character first, ability second." In this respect, ability or talent is something which flows from character, and education, he taught, should be education in character. "What is man's ultimate direction in life?" he asked. His reply was that it is to "look for love, truth, virtue and beauty . . . ." And Suzuki describes this as the central teaching of the Buddha, i.e., to "search for good, the beautiful and love."

And Suzuki was convinced that we should begin the education of character very early on. Such "rearing must start from the day of birth. Here, to my mind, lies the key to the fuller development of man's potentials and abilities." But Suzuki is not promoting impatience, because, as he says, "Ability breeds ability". A seed needs time and stimulation. In fact, the cornerstone of the Suzuki method is good old-fashioned hard work. Ability requires many hours, many days, months and years of practice. As any parent of a would-be musician knows, this often requires great patience. Often, Suzuki would refer to his method as the "mother-tongue method." He was fond of pointing out to everyone who would listen that "all Japanese children speak Japanese." Most who heard this, he tells us, thought him a little bit crazy, or else they expressed themselves in a "so what?" kind of way. But the fact that Japanese children speak their mother-tongue so well, and that all children speak their own languages so fluently, was something that amazed Suzuki. After all, the complexities and subtleties of language are immense. The fact that small children can learn them, he thought, was a very telling point indeed. Here Suzuki echoes an idea more fully developed by the MIT linguistic philosopher Noam Chomsky who also points out the significance that language ability has for learning theory. Just imagine the skills that such a feat require! No doubt, this fact is enough to prove that given the patience and right development, children can accomplish a great deal. But they have to be properly educated.

The method that Suzuki promoted was a philosophy of *education and not of instruction.* Education is more than instruction. And as he himself puts it, "the emphasis has been put on informing and instructing, the actual growth of the child is ignored. There has been no thorough research into how ability is acquired. The word education implies two concepts: to educe, which means to 'bring out, develop from latent or potential existence,' as well as to instruct. But the emphasis in schools is only on the instruction aspect, and the real meaning of education is totally forgotten." Suzuki laments this type of schooling which is reinforced in the giving of test. "Tests," he says, "show the teacher's ability rather than the child's."

"Talent education is life education," and "the life force is beyond human intellect." So it is not only the intellect, but the character and soul that Suzuki wishes his method to educate. It is as Dr. Masaaki Honda has expressed in the book *The Suzuki Concept: An Introduction to a Successful Method for Early Music Education,* "a total human education." And as Suzuki himself expresses in his *Ability Development from Age Zero,* "The fate of a child is in the hands of his parents . . . . The responsibility for education is in the home." At the end of this work, Suzuki warns parents to "please, prepare the best environment for your child. Parent and child should grow together looking towards the future. I pray for your happiness."

At the time of writing, Shinichi Suzuki is a lively and active 94 year old man. His methods continue to be praised world-wide for there incredible success in educating the characters of millions of young people across the globe.

SUZUKI ON WHERE TALENT COMES FROM*

TALENT IS NOT INBORN

Everyone   Has   A   Sprout   of   Talent

Through science we can fly to the moon, yet man has hardly begun to evaluate mankind. This imbalance is a reversal of that which is important and that which is trivial.

We should know our abilities, draw them out, and develop them. When this important duty is neglected, how can we say we live in a civilized world? Man's talent is not inborn.

Some people state: "It is natural to grow up because nature is inborn." "Nothing can be done about a lack of inborn ability." In this fashion, *inborn* is used in good and bad ways. However, please stop and think a bit. Does not *inborn* seem to be used too quickly, too easily, too often?

When we say children have inborn ability, often those children already have nurtured to the age of five or six. When looking at a newborn baby, absolutely nobody can say, "This child will be a talented musician," or, "This child will be a talented literary person."

Saying what is the inborn ability of a five or six year old child cannot be the same as what we mean when speaking of the inborn ability of the infant. Instead, it should be called the results of education, because it is the grown form of a five or six year old that is being observed.

---

* **S o u r c e**: Shinichi Suzuki, **Ability Development from Age Zero** (Athens, Ohio: Ability Development, 1969). Reprinted by permission.

Re-evaluate the school of thought which mistakenly calls the results of education as inborn ability. Start from scratch and think about the talent of man. What kind of person is the newborn child and what kind of talent is hidden within him? This is what I hope to see re-evaluated.

All Japanese Children Speak Japanese!

When the root of this idea occurred to me some twenty-six years ago, I was overwhelmed by the fact that all children in Japan speak Japanese easily.

"Of course they do . . . It's nothing to be surprised about," is what people say to me with skeptical eyes. However, for me it was an enlightening thought. Five and six year old children speak Japanese easily. They speak the difficult dialects of their respective areas such as the Osaka, Aomori, and Kagoshima dialects without any problem. They have the talent to catch the delicate nuances of the Osaka dialect and the ability to master the nasal pronunciation of Aomori and Akita dialects. I was astounded; this ability is no small accomplishment. The children show such a high level of educational possibilities.

Already, at five and six years old, children have developed and internalized language, and I was deeply moved by this discovery which led to my understanding of the education involved in learning the mother tongue.

"Children in Japan speak Japanese so well. How wonderful it is!" I could not help telling every friend I could find. However, whomever I met looked at me suspiciously and said, "What are you talking about? Of course they do."

Nevertheless, my astonishment was clear. All of my thoughts about the Mother Tongue Method began at that time, and my heart overflowed with happiness. Even though people thought I was crazy, I continued to talk about the surprise. I talked about it so much that people began to laugh at me.

I need to explain my surprise at seeing children speak Japanese freely. Such a high level of development seemed to show a successful education method which works unconsciously. I also profited from the strong belief that any child has seeds of ability which can be nurtured as far as the capacity of the brain will allow.

It is so commonplace for children to speak their own language that people tend to ignore it and not really look at the facts. Possibly I was so stimulated when taking note of such a happening because at that time I had been thinking seriously about a new music education method. In a way it was a flash of inspiration.

Mother Tongue Education Is the Best Method

To speak Japanese well, children must develop their language ability to a very high level. One cannot simply say that Japanese children speak Japanese because they are Japanese. If an American spoke Japanese as well as Japanese children do, it would be called a brilliant language ability. Yet a baby starts from scratch at birth and by five or six years of age has internalized the language. Here is a wonderful method of education. The best method in the world is hidden within the mother tongue education, I thought. This event should fit into all education methods. I began to search. Then, at last I decided, "If a child speaks his language fluently, he has developmental possibilities. Other abilities should therefore develop according to the way he is raised."

I asked all mothers, "Does your child speak well?" If the answer is "Yes," then I say, "If so, then that is the evidence that your child can develop excellent abilities with a good education. Have confidence."

Man grows in the same way he is reared. Man can develop to a high level according to the way he is raised. Every child can be educated, but children are not born with education. Knowing this fact will become the basis for insights regarding the nature of mankind.

Ability   Breeds   Ability

Let us think deeply about the way a child learns Japanese. Let us consider, for instance, the number of times a baby hears the Japanese word *Uma*, *Uma* [one of the earliest terms acquired by infants for food], before he begins to say it, and what form the acceleration curve for word acquisition takes until he begins to say other words such as *Mama* or *Papa*. From this we can see that there is an almost uncountable number of times that the baby will hear *Uma Uma* before he is able to say it. Then that ability must grow a great deal more before he can say *Mama* or *Papa* and have a three word vocabulary. While practicing these three words, his ability must again grow a great deal so as to add a fourth word, and yet again to add a fifth. Here we can see that ability is breeding ability.

Since this explanation may be confusing, I will note the standard education procedure here:
"Do you understand?"
"Yes."
"Then let's go on."
Suppose that a baby learned Japanese in the same way?
"If you can say *Uma Uma* today . . . yes, then next . . . . "
The next next day he learns *Mama* and the next *Papa*.

If babies were taught Japanese in this way, no one would say happily that his child had a good memory. If on a particular day one cannot remember how to say the word which was learned the day before, one will only learn to speak the word of the day. With this method, there are big problems.

However, education of Japanese does not involve only learning Japanese in bits and pieces. It also involves developing the *ability to learn* [emphasis added] a language at the same time. Until now, the majority of education methods have concentrated merely upon teaching in bits and pieces instead of nurturing talent.

"If I use this wonderful language education method, surely I will get good results. I shall use the method of ability breeding ability." I began to get moving.

Everyone has a sprout of talent. Developing that sprout into a wonderful ability depends upon how it is cultivated.

Even Tone Deaf Children Can Be Developed

Toshiya Eto was my first experiment. Beginning with him, the number of my pupils grew quickly.

I also taught a six-year-old tone deaf child who was successfully able to develop talent. The tone deaf child was not born that way. When he was a baby, his mother or grandmother sang out-of-tune lullabies to him, and as he heard them he became tone deaf. To cure the child's tone deafness, I used the following method:

It is very difficult to correct tone deafness which has become internalized. Therefore, instead of correcting the old tone deaf gamut [a series of recognized musical notes], I made a new gamut for which I repeated the training over and over again. When the new gamut had been experienced more times than the old gamut, the old gamut gradually wore thin and was erased. That child nurtured his talent so well as to have a recital in Canada. I would like parents to use their perceptive abilities to think about the seed of talent which children have that can be developed to a surprisingly high level.

I would like every parent to experience the surprise that I had when I suddenly realized how easily every child speaks Japanese. I would also have them believe that human ability is nurtured.

If I may say so, parents who say, "My child has no musical talent," or "My child is so weak in literature," are ignorant. If it is known that talent is not inborn but nurtured, then such things cannot be said. The parent who complains about his child is actually announcing to society that he has bad methods for nurturing.

Saying "My child has no talent" is actually the same as saying "I did not educate my child to develop the sprout of his talent."

The Life Force for Environmental Adaptation

One more time I shall give an example that talent is not inborn. Suppose Mozart had been given to me to care for soon after his birth. And further suppose that instead of having the influence of his wonderful musician father, Mozart heard me play an old, bent, out-of-tune record for his lullaby when he cried. Then, if Mozart listened to an out-of-tune record every day and was raised in this environment, Mozart would have internalized the out-of-tuneness and become a tone deaf person.

Even a Mozart had the possibility of becoming tone deaf depending upon the way he was raised. It is not a matter of having inborn musical talent, but rather that of internalizing the talents from the surrounding living environment.

Children Are Seedlings

If adults are considered full-grown plants, then children are seedlings. Unless the seedlings are well cared for, beautiful flowers cannot be expected.

Setting a child aside until elementary school age and then saying that now education begins is like taking a withered or withering sprout and suddenly giving it large amounts of fertilizer, putting it in the sunlight and flooding it with water. It is too late for the withered sprout.

Man has been given the good fortune of a powerful life force and limitless possibilities. It is an inexcusable fault of ours to throw these away unnoticed. Every loving parent has the wish to make his child admirable and happy. However, most parents unconsciously spoil their children or make them unhappy. This happens because they are unable to recognize the powerful life force in their children.

For example, when a child receives poor grades in school, his parents and even his teachers do not doubt that the child is stupid, or not very smart. Yet this same child speaks his own language fluently. How can this fact be explained? The child is not stupid, but he was not reared well.

Suppose we have a normal baby. Further, suppose that we bind the right hand of this baby until he is four years old. If we then try to have the baby use his right hand it will not be developed well. The hand will be useless. The left hand will be well developed and the child will be left-handed. Leaving the talents of a child alone until he is four years old is like binding his right hand.

It is sad that parents all over the world do this very thing without a second thought. The fate of a child is in the hands of his parents. Unfortunately there are many children who are set aside in this manner.

THE MAKING OF A PERSON

Anger Is Unnecessary in Everyday Life

I have often talked about not scolding children, and I would like to expand more fully upon the relationship between anger and ability.

There are some people whose only ability is to display anger and their facial expression always looks angry. Such people may start by becoming angry only occasionally, but eventually as they scold more often it becomes a habit to be angry. The habitually angry person is a veteran scolder and his face colors with anger at the smallest things. What an unhappy person.

I have reflected upon anger and concluded that anger is unnecessary in human life. Practice not being angry instead of developing an ability for anger. I myself practiced not becoming angry for ten years. It changed me from my very roots. What experiences I had!

One day a person challenged me with a knotty problem. He also said some terrible things while my colleagues were in the next room. As I listened to him, I thought that a person capable of saying such things without reason must have grown up in a poor environment. Then instead of feeling anger, I felt sympathy. As his anger progressed, he exposed his poor development and I felt no anger at all. Therefore, I could answer him with kind words of sympathy. Harsh words do not require harsh words. . . .

. . . A child who is raised by a short tempered parent develops a short temper like his parent. He will become enraged with his friends without cause. His ability for anger has been trained every day through the educational method of his parents. Anger is the ability to become angry . . . .

Do Not Rely On General Assumptions

For a long time I have explained that anger is unnecessary in child education. Now we must consider *general assumptions* in relation to ability development.

When we rely on general assumptions, it is normal for us not to use anything but that. However, a common assumption is what someone in the past decided was true and that we take for granted. We should examine these things at least once. There could be an error.

People often say, "I was born to mediocrity," or "Surely I am no genius," and other things about inborn talent. Now everyone understands that this assumption is in error. We must recognize that we are born as wonderful human beings with limitless possibilities.

A person is not born uninteresting. He is trained to be ordinary. When the majority of people are right-handed, left-handed people are considered almost abnormal. However, if left-handed people are abnormal, then right-handed people should also be considered abnormal. When I went to the zoo, I found that monkeys function in a better way. They are ambidextrous. We have made an error in our assumptions . . . .

Personality Is A Talent

Developing one's personality is talked about as if it were an obvious result of education. The problem is that parents and teachers call what is a well developed ability in a child his personality.

Behind *personality development* lies hidden the easy way of educating a child. The child is being educated in something he has already been trained to do well. Then people mistakenly call that ability an inborn ability, and make another error by assuming this.

Last year, sixty university professors came to the Matsumoto Talent Education Research Center. We had a discussion hour in the auditorium. One teacher began by asking my thoughts on personality. I answered by asking what was meant by *personality*. Everyone started laughing because they thought I did not understand the *word*. Then I continued:

"I wonder if trained ability is often mistaken for personality. When people talk about personality, it seems that they are talking about the most well trained ability in the child rather than his personality. Such an ability is not the inborn individuality of the child. If people want to stress having a strong personality, then they should raise children to develop such an admirable personality."

Develop Only Wonderful Characteristics

. . . British people have their own individual characteristics. That is because they were born and raised in Britain. If a British child were brought to Japan at the time of birth and raised by a Japanese parent, then he would not have British-like characteristics. Individuality is an ability, and that child would have Japanese-like characteristics. His body would be that of a Briton, but his actions would have Japanese characteristics.

The foundation of education is to carefully raise children with the ability to be fine human beings without being hindered by their individual characteristics.

Teachers, Have Pride

The frustration of a school teacher is great. It is a terrible situation to have poorly raised children, undeveloped children, children who have been ignored and have become nearly retarded, and well reared children with excellent ability. all together in the same classroom. School teachers are under much strain. They use much effort with little fruition. We must have respect for their behavior.

At the same time, I think that the state should choose people who are worthy of respect to be teachers, and then give them a worthy income. If the present day teachers are superior people, then we can have wonderful dreams for the future of education.

Teachers should have more pride in what they do. In Japan, elementary and junior high schools are like preparatory factories for high school, and high school is like a preparatory factory for the university. Too much emphasis is put on the qualifying entrance exams. Teachers have lost their pride in shaping the adults of tomorrow.

Experienced Teachers Are Necessary

Experienced teachers are needed in elementary and junior high schools. The university is where adults investigate learning, but elementary and junior high schools have the responsibility of developing human beings.

DISCUSSION

We have seen that Suzuki is adamantly convinced that one of the chief errors of adults, teachers and non-teachers alike (or, is it not more accurate to say that, for Suzuki, all adults are teachers to the young?), is the view that talent or ability is somehow inborn or innate within the child. The child's ability, according to Suzuki, is not a matter of how "well endowed" he or she, is genetically speaking. Rather, it is a matter of how well the child is nurtured. The child is like a seed which needs proper planting and nourishment. Everything hangs, that is, on the child's *environment*. Even Mozart, in Suzuki's example, required a special educational environment to develop into the musical genius that we celebrate worldwide.

This environment begins, says Suzuki, as soon as the child is delivered into the world. We cannot wait until the child is ready for formal schooling and let the state or some other systematic structure take over and expect to have good results. If we foolishly wait, it will be "too late for the withered sprout." This implies a very great responsibility for all parents. It is wrong for parents to "set aside" their child thinking that it is the state's job, or society's burden to educate him or her. Education begins immediately, with all of the sights, sounds, feelings and varied perceptions of the newborn infant.

As Suzuki's "mother tongue method" indicates, the need is for constant and consistent repetition, day after day, month after month, year after year. The child does not become educated once and for all and all of a sudden (as if it is over and done with). Education is a life-long process, and on-going.

As Suzuki makes clear, we are talking about the development of *character*, the *making of a person*! What could be more important? What is more deserving of our constant attention? It can therefore be said, without exaggeration, that teachers are person-makers. We can see, then, why Suzuki asks teachers to "have more pride in what they do." With this understanding, one can reasonably ask; is their any more noble profession than teaching?

Discussion Questions

1. Do you agree with Suzuki's central theme that talent or ability is not inborn? Explain your answer. Give examples if you can.

2. Do you agree with him that character comes before ability? Explain why or why not.

3. Is Suzuki's distinction between "education" and "instruction" valid? Discuss the difference.

4. Is it true that tests only test the ability of the teacher rather than the child? Discuss.

5. How would Suzuki's methods be incorporated into the classroom? Give some specific examples. Would they work? Are they practical? Explain.

CHAPTER FIFTEEN

JEAN PIAGET

There are few people in the history of psychology whose command of their subject matter goes beyond that of their own immediate discipline. Jean Piaget, however, could easily lay claim to expertise in philosophy with his treatise on genetic epistemology (origins of the intellect); logic and mathematics, with experiments on space, time, chance, and the relationship of the lattice and group to the structure of human thought; biology and natural science as a world renown expert on mollusks; and child cognitive psychology, where he systematically formulated a theory of intellectual development spanning the years from birth to adolescence. A man of brilliant intellect, Piaget often shifted from topic to topic in the course of his writings, which makes reading him somewhat difficult for the average undergraduate. Nevertheless, his work is tremendously important to education and psychology, and his theories are required reading for most students of the social sciences. Before considering his ideas on cognitive development, we first examine his life.

Jean Piaget was born in Neuchatel, Switzerland on August 9, 1896. Even as a young child he was studious, serious, and demonstrated talents as an astute observer and recorder of information. His first publication came at the age of ten, and at age twelve he served after school as a volunteer assistant to the director of the local museum of natural history. At the suggestion of a close uncle, he began reading philosophy, awakening within him an interest into the study of knowledge, or epistemology. What were the origins of knowledge? How does one know if they really know something? How are the mind and the body collectively involved in this process? These and related questions fascinated and puzzled Piaget. He became convinced that the logic and structure of the science of biology might successfully be applied to the study of knowledge. Over the next four years he published more than twenty short papers, and in 1916 he received his undergraduate degree in natural science from the University of Neuchatel. Only two short years later, at the age of 22, he completed his dissertation on a study of mollusks on Switzerland, and was awarded the Doctor of Philosophy in Biology.

As we have just seen, Piaget did extensive reading in fields outside of the natural sciences, and was especially intrigued with philosophy and psychology. His keen mind was already searching for an avenue for integration of these diverse ideas and facts. How could the methods of science be used to answer the questions of philosophy? It was to be the field of Developmental Psychology that Piaget would eventually turn to in his quest to unite the various parts into the whole.

After receiving his Doctorate, Piaget went to Zurich where he was introduced to the ideas of Sigmund Freud, Carl Jung and others within the Psychoanalytic tradition. Piaget was sympathetic to many of these ideas, and was probably also influenced by the "talking method" of Freud, who was able to gain tremendous insights into his patients through careful dialogue and interpretation. Piaget was later to adopt a very similar approach, known as the clinical interview method, where the direction of the interview was dictated by the responses of the child, rather than by any pre-imposed structure. While many of his critics opposed his lack of standardized methods of investigation, Piaget felt that the diversity and complexity of the subject matter necessitated this type of approach.

A significant turning point in Piaget's life came in 1920, when he accepted a position at the Alfred Binet Laboratory in

Paris. Binet had earlier devised a test of intelligence that could discriminate between average, gifted and slow to learn students (with few modifications, the Standford Binet of today is quite similar to the original). While working with children in an effort to standardize the test, Piaget became interested in the logic and reasoning behind the child's incorrect responses. Rather than to simply catalog what the child knew (which was the purpose of the Binet test), Piaget wanted to explore the reasons behind the child's "wrong" answers. He became convinced that older children were not more intelligent than younger ones, but were qualitatively different, meaning that they had available to them systems of logic and cognitive representations that younger children had not yet acquired. The next question of course was to discover how and when these systems developed during the lifetime of the child.

Piaget was to spend the majority of his life in pursuit of the answers to these questions. In 1921, Piaget accepted the post of Director of Research at the Rousseau Institute in Geneva. During the next six decades he published over thirty books and numerous articles detailing his results in the evolution of childhood thought. These books covered a variety of topics, including language, moral reasoning, and ideas related to chance. In 1942 Albert Einstein suggested that Piaget investigate the child's development into notions of space, time and motion, which did in fact yield valuable information into the genesis of these concepts. Piaget was appointed Professor of History of Scientific Thought at the University of Geneva, and awarded Honorary Doctorates at Harvard, the Sorbonne in Paris, and the University of Brazil.

In 1956, Piaget was able to realize a project that he had contemplated for some time. With the assistance of Geneva University, a Center for Genetic Epistemology was created. The purpose of the Center was to bring together scholars from various fields to collectively investigate a selected topic. Members of the research team would approach the problem from their own perspective, and the results of these studies would then be discussed and published in a series of monographs in the journal *Studies in Genetic Epistemology.*

Piaget was a tireless and dedicated researcher who continued to pursue his interests well into his later years. Many of his most important observations came from the study of his own three children. During this time he would carefully record their behaviors and words, and then analyze his findings with exacting detail. The following example is typical of the care and attention Piaget demonstrated in his work: "At 1; 0 (10) T. was looking at a box of matches which I was holding on its end and alternately opening and closing. Showing great delight, he watched with great attention and imitated the box in three ways. 1. He opened and closed his right hand, keeping his eyes on the box. 2. He said 'tff, tff' to reproduce the sound the box made. 3. He reacted like L. at 1; 4 (0) by opening and closing his mouth...." *(Play, Dreams and Imitation,* page 66). Piaget's books are filled with thousands of examples of observation followed by interpretation of actions. Many of his original experiments are still reproduced in assignments given to undergraduate students in Psychology. After a lifetime of dedicated research, Piaget died on September 16, 1980. In the last paragraph of his obituary, written by his fried David Elkind, we find these simple words: "Jean Piaget was a man of heroic, yes of epic, proportions. And yet, as I have tried to suggest here, he was warmly human too." *(The American Psychologist,* August 1981).

We can now consider the essential features of Piaget's theory. To begin with, it is a theory of cognitive development, or in more familiar words, the growth of intelligence within the child. Piaget stresses that intellectual growth is active in nature, which is to say that the child is not merely a passive recipient of information. According to Piaget, development occurs at all ages by the interaction of two fundamental processes, which he calls assimilation and accommodation. Assimilation involves taking information from the world through the senses and making a comparison to the information already stored in the brain. The brain contains numerous schema, or mental representations, which allow each of us to interpret and understand our reality. Now, if our schema can account for the current information as supplied by assimilation, no further work is necessary; we understand the world as it is presented. However, if the new information is foreign or discrepant from what we currently know (our schemata), we must either create a new schema, or enlarge or modify an existing schema. This active component of intelligence is referred to as accommodation.

An example will help to clarify these three terms. A four year old child is looking at a chair. The child must first assimilate this image to the available schema to see if a match can be found. Most likely the search will result in the child's understanding of the object; it "fits" his representation of what a chair is. But, say that the same child is viewing a bean bag chair for the first time. This image does not nicely fit into his current schema of chair, and this being the case he is not sure of the reality that he sees. When it is explained to him that indeed this is a form of a chair, he must accommodate his schema to incorporate the new object. The concept (schema) of chair has been enlarged; not all chairs are rigid and well formed, and not all chairs are made of wood or plastic, might be the results of the accommodation. Because of accommodation, the mental representation of chair has grown, and cognitive growth has also, therefore, occurred.

Assimilation and accommodation operate continuously within the individual to bring about intellectual adaptation. Cognitive growth occurs as new schema are modified or created to fit the demands of reality. However, individuals at different ages understand their world in qualitatively different ways. Piaget refers to this phenomena as a stage sequence of development. During the course of his work, Piaget described the characteristics of four major stages that all individuals pass through from birth to adolescence. We can now examine briefly the major aspects of each stage.

Beginning at birth and lasting for roughly the first two years of life is the <u>Sensory Motor Stage</u>. Infants are for the most part non-verbal, yet a tremendous amount of learning is taking place at this time. Infants learn by taking information in through their senses, comparing it with what they already know (assimilation), and create or enlarge their representations of the world (accommodation). A familiar example might be a six month old girl playing with a rattle. Through her play she is learning about texture, sound, hardness, taste, graspability, the relationship of force to the sensation of loudness, and so on. Quite an impressive accomplishment for a baby, but such is the active nature of Sensory Motory learning. As the child emerges into the beginnings of language, she will be able to label her representations (doggie, mama, rattle), and will be ready to move into the next major stage of cognitive growth, that of Pre-operations.

Between the ages of approximately two and six, the child enters into the <u>Pre-operational stage</u>. While becoming more comfortable with language, the child is still largely dominated by the direct and immediate sensations of the world. For example, a four year old child might believe that a fixed amount of liquid in a wide glass changes in amount when it is poured into a tall slender glass. To the child, because it looks taller, it has more quantity. This failure to conserve the quantity of a liquid is typical of children at this age. They have not yet acquired the mental flexibility to allow them to solve this type of problem, hence the term "Pre-operational". Additionally, most children at this age are egocentric, assuming that other people know and understand the world in the same way that they do. A young child might not understand how a person can be sleepy when they are wide awake. During this time the child is gradually coming to understand the world around him, but it will not be until the next stage that the beginnings of logical thought can be applied to this world.

Piaget refers to his third stage as <u>Concrete Operations</u>, from about seven to eleven years. Children at this level have had numerous experiences with their social contacts, and have lost their egocentricity. More importantly for Piaget, the child can now use mental operations to make logical inferences about the world. The most important of these cognitive operations is reversibility, whose operation implies identity. Given the same liquid conservation problem that we presented earlier, the Concrete Operational person will respond that the amount of liquid remains constant, despite a change in its appearance. Further, they will argue that one could verify this by undoing the process (reversibility); an action which has had this inverse operation applied must necessarily return to its original state. We can clearly see how important the attainment of this concept is for the child's later understanding of mathematics, physics and chemistry.

Even at this level, however, the child will still run into problems within the areas of abstraction and hypothetical thought. It is one thing to apply an operation to an object; it is another to apply an operation to another operation. One can for example think about going shopping, or one can think about the fact that they are thinking about going shopping. This stage of development, the final one in Piaget's theory, is called <u>Formal Operations</u>. At this stage, which runs from twelve to eighteen, the adolescent can truly begin to appreciate the intangible, hypothetical nature of certain aspects of the world. As a common example, most adolescents now begin to seriously think about their lives after high school graduation. They envision many possibilities (college, marriage, employment, armed services), make inferences about how their life might be by adopting one or more of these roles, and even give thought to possibilities within possibilities (college as a psychology major versus college as a business major).

It should again be emphasized that at all stages, the process of cognitive growth is the same, that is the interplay between assimilation and accommodation. Individuals are active learners, and people at different stages are qualitatively different from one another. In the following reading taken from *The Child and Reality*, Piaget discusses these and related ideas, and hints at the direction that formal education should take in order to best serve the cognitive needs of the individual.

PIAGET ON THE INTELLECTUAL DEVELOPMENT OF THE CHILD*

Child development is a temporal operation par excellence. I will try to offer some data needed to understand this situation.

More specifically, I will focus on two points. The first is the necessary role of time in the life cycle. Any development-psychological as well as biological--supposes duration, and the childhood lasts longer as the species becomes more advanced; the childhood of a kitten and that of a chick are much shorter than that of the human infant since the human infant has much more to learn. This is what I shall try to show in these pages.

The second point is formulated in the questions: Does the life cycle express a basic biological rhythm, an ineluctable law? Does civilization modify this rhythm and to what extent? In other words, is it possible to increase or decrease this temporal development?

To discuss these two points I have in mind only the truly psychological development of the child as opposed to his school development or to his family development; that is, I will above all stress the spontaneous aspect of this development, though I will limit myself to the purely intellectual and cognitive development.

Actually we can distinguish two aspects in the child's intellectual development. On the one hand, we have what can be called the psychosocial aspect, that is, everything the child receives from without and learns in general by family, school,

---

* **Source**: Jean Piaget, *"Time and the Intellectual Development of the Child"*, in his **The Child and Reality** (New York: Penguin Books, 1976).   Reprinted by permission.

educative transmission. On the other there is the development of the intelligence itself--what the child learns by himself, what none can teach him and he must discover alone; and it is essentially this development which takes time.

Let us immediately take two cases. In a group of objects, for example a bouquet of flowers where you count six primroses and six flowers which are not primroses, you would discover that there are more flowers than primroses, that the whole is greater than the part. This seems so obvious that no one would think of teaching it to a child. And yet, as we will see, he needs years to discover such a law.

Another common case concerns transitivity. If a stick compared to another is equal to it, and if this second stick is equal to a third, is the first-which I will hide under the table-equal to the third? Does A equal C if A equals B and B equals C? Again this is completely obvious to us; no one would imagine teaching this to a child. But he needs, as we will see, almost seven years to discover such logical laws.

Thus what I am going to discuss is the spontaneous aspect of intelligence, and it is the only one I will mention because I am only a Psychologist and not an educator; also because from the viewpoint of time, it is precisely this spontaneous development which forms the obvious and necessary condition for the school development.

In our classes at Geneva, it is only around the age of eleven that we begin to teach the notion of proportion. Why not earlier? Obviously, if the child could learn it earlier, the school program would have included the initiation to proportions for those aged nine or even seven. If the child has to wait until he is eleven, the reason is that this notion supposes all kinds of complex operations. A proportion is a relation among relations. To understand a relation of relations, a single relation must first be understood. The whole logic of relations must first be construed, after which this logic of relations must be applied to the logic of numbers. There is a vast set of operations which remain implicit; they are not distinguished at the outset and are hidden beneath this notion of proportion. This example, one of a hundred others possible, shows how psychosocial development is subordinated to spontaneous and psychological development.

I will thus limit myself to this aspect of development and begin at once with a concrete example.   It concerns an experiment we did some time ago in Geneva.   Offer a child two small balls of clay measuring from three to four centimeters in diameter.   The child verifies that they are similar in volume, weight, everything.   Ask him to change one of the clay balls into a sausage, to flatten it into a cake, or to divide it into small sections.   Then ask him three questions.

First: Has the amount of matter remained the same?

Naturally, you will use a child's language.   Ask him if there is the same amount of clay once the ball has been formed into a sausage, or simply if there is more or less clay than before.

Amount of matter, conservation of matter...oddly enough, it is usually not until the age of eight that seventy-five percent of children solve this problem.   This is only an average.   If you conduct the experiment with your own children, you will naturally have a more precocious result, for in relation to the average, your children are certainly ahead.   But for the average it is eight years.

Second: Has the weight remained the same?

Offer the child a small scale.   If I place the ball of clay on one scale and the sausage on the other, with the understanding that the sausage comes from the ball only by change of form, is the weight going to be the same?

⟶ The notion of the conservation of weight is not acquired until about the age of nine or ten, about ten for seventy-five percent of children, that is, at a lag of two years after acquiring the notion of substances.

Third: Has the volume remained the same? Instead of discussing volume, as the term is difficult, use an indirect method. Immerse the ball in a glass of water; show that the water rises because the ball takes it place. Then ask if the sausage immersed in the glass of water is going to take the same space, that is, make the water rise the same distance.

⟶ This problem is not solved till the age of twelve. Thus there is a further lag of two years after solving the problem of the conservation of weight.

Let us quickly see the arguments of those who have no notion of conservation, or of substance, or of weight, or of volume. The argument is always the same. The child will say, "First it was round, then you lengthened the stuff. The moment you made it longer, there is more." He looks at one of the dimensions and forgets the other. The striking thing in this reasoning is that he considers the configuration of the beginning, the configuration of the end, but he fails to consider the transformation itself. He forgets that one thing has been changed into another; he compares the ball seen at the beginning with its state at the end, and he replies, "No, it is longer and therefore there is more of it."

He then discovers that it is the same substance, the same quantity of material. Yet he will say, after the lag of the two years I mentioned and with the same arguments, "It is longer and therefore heavier."

Let us see what the arguments are which lead to the notion of the conservation. They are always the same and three in number.

The first argument is what I will call the argument of identity. The child will say, "But nothing has been removed, nothing added, so therefore it is the same thing, the same quantity of material." And about the age of eight, he finds it so unusual that one should ask him such an easy question that he smiles, shrugs his shoulders, never thinking that a year earlier he would have given a different answer. He will therefore say, "It's the same thing because you have neither removed or added anything. But as for the weight, it is longer and therefore heavier." And we have the former argument.

Second argument: reversibility. The child will say, "You have lengthened the matter, you merely have to form it into a ball again and you will see that it is the same thing."

Third argument: compensation. The child will say, "It has been increased in length, that's understood, there is more, but at the same time, it is thinner. The material is more on one side but less on the other. Consequently there is compensation and it's the same thing."

These simple facts at once allow us to make two statements relative to time, by distinguishing in time two fundamental areas: on the one hand, duration, and on the other, order of succession of the events--duration being only the interval between orders of succession.

1. First of all, time is necessary for duration. For seventy-five percent of children, one must wait eight years for the notion of the conservation of substance, and ten for that of weight. Even every adult has not acquired the notion of the conservation of weight. Spencer in his *Treatise on Sociology* tells the story of a woman who preferred to travel with a long piece of luggage rather than a square one because she thought that her dresses when spread out in the long case weighed less than when folded in the square case. As for the concept of volume, one must wait twelve years.

These results occur not only in Geneva--the experiments which we did in Geneva between 1937 and 1940 were resumed in France, Poland, England, and the United States, Canada, Iran, and even in Aden, on the banks of the Red Sea. These same stages were found everywhere. But on average no earlier understanding was found with the children of Geneva, even those of a distinguished rank, as we shall soon see. In other words, there is a minimum age for understanding these concepts except, of course, for certain selected social groups, such as children of the talented.

Can one accelerate such development by learning? This is the question that was asked by one of our colleagues, the Norwegian psychologist Jan Smedslund, at our Center of Genetic Epistemology. He tried to hasten acquisition of the notion of conservation of weight through certain instruction-in the American sense of the term-that is, by external reinforcement, for example by reading the result on the scale. But we must first understand that the acquisition of the notion of conservation supposes an entire logic, and entire reasoning based on the transformations themselves, and consequently on the notion of reversibility-this reversibility which the child himself brings to mind when he reaches the notion of conservation. And above all, this notion of conservation supposes transitivity: A state A of the ball being equal to a state B, the state B being equal to a state C, the state A will be equal to the state C. There is a correlation between these various operations. Smedslund began by verifying this correlation and he found a very significant correlation on the subjects studied between the notion of conservation on one side and that of transitivity on the other. He then turned to learning experiences: After each reply, he showed the child the results on the scale which indicated that the weight was the same. After two or three times, the child constantly repeated, "It will always be the same weight, it will again be the same weight." etc.

There will thus be learning of the result. But what is chiefly interesting is that this learning of the result is limited to this result; in other words, when Smedslund turned to the learning of transitivity (which is another matter, since transitivity is part of the logical framework leading to this result), he was unable to obtain learning for this transitivity despite the findings repeated on the scale of A=C, A=B and B=C. Thus it is one thing to learn a result and another to form an intellectual instrument, a logic required to construct such a result. Such a new reasoning instrument is not formed in a few days. That is what this experiment proves....

This brings us to the theory of the stages of development. Development is achieved by successive levels and stages. In this development which I am going to describe briefly, we distinguish four important stages.

First, we have a stage, before about age eighteen months, which precedes speech and which we will call that of the sensorimotor intelligence. Secondly, we have a stage which begins with speech and lasts for about seven or eight years. We will call this the period of representation, but is preoperatory in the sense that I will soon define. Then, between about seven and twelve, we will distinguish a third period which we will call that of concrete operations. And finally, after twelve years, there is the stage of propositional or formal operations.

Thus we distinguish successive stages. Let us note that these stages are precisely characterized by their set order of succession. They are not stages which can be given a constant chronological date. On the contrary, the ages can vary from one society to another, as we will see at the close of this report. But there is a constant order of succession. It is always the same and for the reasons we have just glimpsed; that is, in order to reach a certain stage, previous steps must be taken. The prestructures and previous substructures which make for further advance must be constructed.

Thus we reach a hierarchy of structures which are built in a certain order of integration and which moreover, interestingly enough, appear at senescense to disintegrate in the reverse order, as the fine work carried out by Dr. Ajuriaguerra and his colleagues seems to show in the present state of their research.

Let us rapidly describe these stages to show why time is necessary, and why so much time is required to reach these notions which are as obvious and simple as those I have used as examples.

Let us begin with the period of sensorimotor intelligence. There is intelligence before speech, but there is not thought before speech. In this respect, let us distinguish intelligence and thought. Intelligence for the child is the solution of a new problem, in the coordination of the means to reach a certain goal which is not accessible in an immediate manner; whereas thought is interiorized intelligence no longer based on direct action but on a symbolism, and other means, which makes it possible to represent what the sensorimotor intelligence, on the contrary, is going to grasp directly....

...Let us give two examples. First, there is the notion of the permanent object. At first glance, nothing is more simple. The philosopher Meyerson believed that the permanence of the object was given at the very outset of perception, and that there was no way of perceiving an object without believing it to be permanent. Here the infant enlightens us. Take an infant of five or six months after the coordination of vision and prehension, that is, when he can begin to grasp the objects he sees. Offer him an object which interests him, for example a watch. Place it before him on the table and he reaches out to grasp the object.

Screen the object, for example with a piece of cloth. You will see that the infant simply withdraws his hand if the object is not important to him or becomes angry if the object has some special interest for him, for example if it is his feeding bottle. But he does not think of raising the cloth to find the object behind it. And this is not because he does not know how to move a cloth from an object. If you place the cloth on his face, he very well knows how to remove it at once, whereas he does not know how to look behind to find the object. Thus everything happens as though the object, once it has disappeared from the field of perception, were reabsorbed, had lost all existence, had not yet acquired that substantiality which, as we have seen, requires eight years to reach its quantitive characteristic of conservation. The outer world is only a series of moving pictures which appear and disappear, the most interesting of which can reappear when one knows very well how to manage it (for example crying long enough if it is a question of someone whose return is desired). But these are only moving pictures without substantiality or permanence and, above all, without localization.

Second stage: You will see the infant raise the cloth to find the object hidden behind. But the following control shows that the entire notion has not really been acquired. Place the object on the infant's right, then hide it; he is going to look for it. Then remove it from him, pass it slowly before his eyes, and place it at his left. (Here we are talking of an infant of nine or ten months.) After seeing the object disappear at his left, the infant will at once look for it at his right where he found it the first time. Thus here there is only a semipermanence without localization. The infant is going to look where the action of looking proved successful the first time and independently of the mobility of the object....

...I will move on to discuss the period of the preoperatory representation. At about a year and a half or two years, an important event occurs in the child's intellectual development. It is then that there appears the capacity to represent something with something else, which is known as the symbolical function. One form of symbolical function is speech, a system of social signs as opposed to individual symbols. But simultaneous with this speech, there are other manifestations of the symbolical function. A second form is play which becomes symbolical: representing something by means of an object or of a gesture. Until then play was only a play of motor exercises, whereas after about a year and a half, for example, the child really begins to play. One of my children passed around a seashell in a box while saying "meow" because a moment earlier he had seen a cat on a wall. In this case the symbol is obvious, since the child had no other word at his disposal. What is new, however, is to represent something with something else.

A third form of symbolism can be a gestural system of symbolics, for example in the postponed imitation.

A fourth form will be the beginning of the mental picture or interiorized imitation.

Thus there exists a set of symbolizers which appear at the level and which make thought possible, thought being, I repeat, a system of interiorized action and leading to those particular actions which we will call operations, reversible actions and actions coordinating one to another into a total system about which I will shortly have a few words to say.

A situation is presented there which poses the problem of time in the most acute manner. Why do the logical structures, the reversible operations which we have just characterized, and the notion of conservation which we have mentioned, not appear the moment there is speech and the moment there is symbolical function? Why must we wait eight years to acquire the invariant of substance and more so for the other notions instead of their appearing the moment there is symbolical function, that is, the possibility of thought and not simply material action? For the basic reason that the actions that have allowed for certain results on the ground of material effectivity cannot be interiorized any further in an immediate manner, and that it is a matter of relearning on the level of thought what has already been learned on the level of action. Actually this interiorization is a new structuration; it is not simply a translation but a restructuration with a lag which takes a considerable time....

...I now come to the level of concrete operations, at an average age of about seven years in our civilizations. But we will see that there are delays or increases due to the action of social life. About the age of seven, a fundamental turning point is noted in a child's development. He becomes capable of certain logic; he becomes capable of coordinating operations in the sense of reversibility, in the sense of the total system of which I will soon give one or two examples. This period coincides with the beginning of elementary schooling. Here again I believe that the psychological factor is a decisive one. If this level of the concrete operations came earlier, elementary schooling would begin earlier. This is not possible before a certain level of elaboration has been achieved, and I shall now try to give its characteristics.

Let us note at once that the operations of thought, on this level, are not identical to what is our own logic or to what adolescent logic will become. Adolescent logic--and our logic-- is essentially a logic of speech. In other words, we are capable --and the adolescent becomes so as early as the age of twelve or fifteen--of reasoning on propositional, verbal statements. We are capable of manipulating propositions, of reasoning by placing ourselves in the viewpoints of others without believing the propositions on which we reason. We are capable of manipulating them in a formal and hypothetico-deductive manner.

As we will see, this logic requires much time to be constructed. Before this logic, a previous stage must be passed, and this is what I will call the period of concrete operations. This previous period is that of a logic which is not based on verbal statements but only on the objects themselves, the manipulable objects. This will be a logic of classifications because objects can be collected all together or in classifications; or else it will be a logic of relations because objects can be combined according to their different relations; or else it will be a logic of numbers because objects can be materially counted by manipulating them. This will thus be a logic of classifications, relations, and numbers, and not yet a logic of propositions. Nevertheless we are dealing with a logic, in the sense that for the first time we are in the presence of operations that can be reversed--for example addition, which is the same operation as subtraction but in a reversed way. It is a logic in the sense that the operations are coordinated, grouped in whole systems which have their laws in terms of totalities. And we must very strongly insist on the necessity of these whole structures for the development of thought.

A number, for example, does not exist in an isolated state. What is given is a series of numbers, that is, an organized system which is the unit plus the unit, and so forth. A logical classification, a concept, does not exist in an isolated state. What is given is the total system which we will call a classification. Likewise a "greater than..." relation of comparison does not exist in the isolated state; it is part of a whole structure we will call the seriation, which consists in arranging the elements according to the same relation.

It is these structures which are constructed as early as the age of seven, and from this moment on the notions of conservation become possible....

...2. Classification. This is acquired only about the age of seven or eight, if you take as criteria of classification the inclusion of a subcategory in a category, that is the understanding of the fact that a part is smaller than the whole. This can appear extraordinary and yet it is true. Give a child flowers which include six primroses and six other flowers. Ask him, "Are all the primroses flowers?" He'll reply, "Of course; yes." "Are all the flowers primroses?" His reply, "Of course not." "Are there more primroses on this table or more flowers?" The child will look, then reply, "There are more primroses," or he will say, "It's the same thing because there are six on one side and six on the other."

"But you just told me that primroses are flowers. Are there more flowers or more primroses?"

The flowers mean to him what remains after the primroses; this is not the inclusion of the part in the whole but the comparison of a part with the other part.

This is interesting as a sign of concrete operations. Note that with flowers, this problem is solved about the age of eight. But if you take animals, the solution comes later. Ask a child, "Are all animals birds?"

"Certainly not. There are snails, horses...."

"Are all birds animals?"

"Certainly."

"Well, if you look out the window, are there more birds or more animals?"

"I don't know. You'd have to go and count them."

It is impossible therefore to deduct the inclusion of the subcategory in the category simply by the manipulations of the "all" and "some." And this is probably because the flowers can be gathered in bouquets. This is an easy concrete operation, whereas to go and make a bouquet of swallows becomes more complicated; it is not manipulable.

I come finally to the formal operations at about the age of twelve and with fourteen to fifteen years of age as equilibrium level.

This concerns a final stage during which the child not only becomes capable of reasoning and of deducting on manipulable objects, like sticks to arrange, numbers of objects to collect, etc., but he also becomes capable of logic and of deductive reasoning on theories and propositions. A new logic, a whole set of specific operations are superimposed on the preceding ones and this can be called the logic of propositions. Actually this supposes two fundamental new characteristics. First there is the combinatory. Until now everything was done gradually by a series of interlockings; whereas the combinatory connect any element with any other. Here then is a new characteristic based on a kind of classification of all the classifications or seriation of all the seriations. The logic of propositions will suppose, moreover, the combination in a unique system of the different groupments which until now were based either on reciprocity or on inversion, on the different forms of reversibility (group of the four transformations: inversion, reciprocity, correlativity, identity). Thus we are in the presence of a completion which, in our societies, is not noted until about the age of fourteen or fifteen and which takes such a long time, because, to arrive at this point, the child must go through all kinds of stages, each being necessary to the achievement of the following one....

...Here therefore is the state of fact: there are variations in the rapidity and duration of the development. How to interpret them? The development, of which I have tried to make a very schematic and very concise list, can be explained by different factors.

I distinguish four.

First factor: heredity, internal maturation. This factor can certainly be retained from every viewpoint, but is insufficient because it never occurs in the pure or isolated state. If a maturation effect intervenes everywhere, it remains dissociable from the effects of the exercise of learning or of experience. Thus heredity is not a factor which acts alone or which can be isolated psychologically.

Second factor: the physical experience, the action of objects.   It again forms an essential factor which cannot be underestimated but which likewise is insufficient.   Child logic especially is not drawn from the experience of objects, it is drawn from the actions which effect the objects.   This is not the same; that is, the part of the child's activity is fundamental, and here, the experience drawn from the object is insufficient.

Third factor: social transmission, the educative factor in the large sense.   Naturally a determining factor in development, it alone is insufficient for the obvious reason that if a transmission is possible between adult and child or between the social milieu and the educated child, the child must assimilate what one is trying to inculcate in him from without.   This assimilation is always conditioned by the laws of the partially spontaneous development, a few examples of which I have given.

Let us recall in regard to this the inclusion of the subcategory in the category, the part smaller than the whole. Speech contains many cases in which the inclusion is marked in a completely explicit manner by the words themselves.   But this does not enter the child's mind so long as the operation is not constructed on the level of the interiorized actions.   For example, I once studied--this was another Burt test--a test in which it was a question of determining the color of a bouquet of flowers, considering the following statement:

A boy says to his sisters, "Some of my flowers are buttercups." (I had even simplified by saying, "Some of my flowers are yellow.") The first sister replied, "Then your bouquet is yellow, it is completely yellow."   The second replied, "Part of your flowers are yellow"; and the third replied, "None of your flowers is yellow."   Young French children--this was a study made in Paris--until the ages of nine and ten replied:

"The first two are right because they say the same thing. The first said, 'Your whole bouquet is yellow' and the second, 'some of your flowers are yellow.' That's the same thing; that means that there are some yellow flowers and that they are all yellow." In other words, the genitive partitive, the relation of the part to the whole, was not understood by speech for lack of structuration of the inclusion.

I would like to speak of a fourth factor which I will call the factor of equilibrium. From the moment when there are three factors, there must already be a balance among them; but further, in intellectual development, a fundamental factor intervenes. The fact is that a discovery, a new notion, a statement, etc., must balance with the others. A whole play of regulation and of compensation is required to result in a coherence. I take the word equilibrium not in a static sense but in that of a progressive equilibration, the equilibrium being the compensation by reaction of the child to the outer disturbances, a compensation which leads to the operatory reversibility at the end of this development.

Equilibrium appears to me to be the fundamental factor of this development. We then understand both the possibility of acceleration and at the same time the impossibility of an increase going beyond certain limits.

The possibility of acceleration is given in the facts which I previously indicated, but theoretically, if the development is above all a matter of equilibrium, because a balance can regulate itself more or less rapidly according to the child's activity, it is not regulated automatically like a hereditary process which would be subjected from within.

If we compare to the young Greeks of the time when Socrates, Plato, and Aristotle invented the formal or propositional operations of our Western logic, our young contemporaries, who have to assimilate not only the logic of proportions but all the knowledge acquired by Descartes,

Galileo, Newton, and others, a hypothesis must be made that there is a considerable increase in the course of childhood until the level of adolescence.

Balance takes time, this we agree, but the equilibration can be more or less rapid. Nevertheless this acceleration cannot grow indefinitely, and it is here that I will end. I do not believe that there is even an advantage in attempting to increase child development beyond certain limits. Balance takes time and everyone portions this in his own way. Too much increase runs the risk of interrupting the balance. The ideal of education is not to teach the maximum, to maximize the results, but above all to learn to learn, to learn to develop, and to learn to continue to develop after leaving school.

DISCUSSION

Piaget's astute observations concerning the development of intelligence in children clearly have implications for the classroom. His theories point out the individual differences in development. It also follows, that a child cannot benefit from being taught a skill or lesson too early, i.e., before the proper level of maturation.

Focusing on the stages will alert the teacher to how the child constructs reality at different levels. For Piaget, it is the process itself, and not the actual results of this development that demand attention. Simply because a child is aware of a certain result, is no guarantee that he or she understands the reasoning or logic that led up to the conclusion. In addition, specific results (e.g., from the liquid conservation tests) do not necessarily generalize to other similar situations (such as conservation of weight or volume).

Perhaps the major message of the reading is that the classroom teacher should appreciate the limits and capacities of each individual child, and recognize the stage sequences as they unfold within the child. The teaching of the child rests not only on the accumulation of factual knowledge, but on the appreciation and understanding of the ways in which the child operates.

Discussion Questions

1. Name three cognitive strategies that a child might employ to solve a conservation problem.

2. Referring to question one, would Piaget say that these three processes can be taught to the child in the traditional sense of the word? Explain your answer.

3. Briefly describe the major aspects of Cognitive Development at each of the four stages.

4. Discuss how schema, assimilation, and accommodation are interrelated.

5. Piaget's theory suggests that children learn by actively participating in their environment. Name several specific ways you might encourage active learning in your classroom.

CHAPTER SIXTEEN

CONCLUSION

We have now completed the journey through ideas about education coming from some of the most talented minds in world history. Our journey has covered more than twenty-five centuries and many countries. We have read representatives from ancient *China* (Confucius) and *Greece* (Plato); from *England* (Locke) *France* (Rousseau) and *Switzerland* (Piaget); from *America* (Dewey, James, Skinner, Rogers, Mann and Washington) and *Japan* (Suzuki); from *Germany* (Herbart) and *Italy* (Montessori). These educators come to us from different times and places, different backgrounds and beliefs. But when it comes to the topics of teaching and learning, they offer us ideas which are in essential agreement concerning the nature, goals and purposes of education. Along the way the reader has noticed, no doubt, some disagreements. Plato and Locke, for example, are at odds when it comes to the basic structure of the mind. Plato proposed the *rationalistic* view, claiming that the mind is born with innate information "written on it" so to speak, while Locke offered the *empiricist* model where innate ideas are rejected for the "tabula rasa" or clean slate theory. There were basic disagreements, too, for instance, between Confucius and Dewey, about the relative importance of the classics. Confucius called his students *back* to the "Ancients" so that their wisdom could be "transmitted", and Dewey looked more towards the *future* for a more "progressive" approach. And many of our thinkers would disagree with Rousseau's rather negative view of *society* and its true role in our lives. These and many other disagreements could be raised for discussion and debate. Part of what we offer in this text is the opportunity to have a dialogue of and about these very things. But behind these differences there lies a vast fabric of agreement. It is the point of view of the authors of this text that the reader is better served by an emphasis on the many, basic similarities between the thinkers we have studied. The following is meant, therefore, as a highlight of *some* of these.

1. Education as Foundation:

First and foremost, each of our thinkers is convinced of the absolute foundational importance of education in general. Education, they believe, is not a topic that a society can take lightly or in roundabout fashion. It is not something the state can afford to "get around to" when supposed "more important" matters are solved. Education is *foundational*, they argue, in the way in which any house or building requires a system of support--quite literally, a foundation! Without a sound foundation, the structure will collapse. Quite literally, these thinkers believe that without a sound educational system, the society supported by it will crumble.

2. Society as Benefactor:

This leads logically to a second primary agreement: it is society which is the chief benefactor of education. Our thinkers are unwavering in their support for this idea. Society can make no more important investment than the one it makes on education. In fact, education is the major vehicle for the perpetuation and growth of a society. It is in our educational systems, where our young citizens learn about the history, development, structure, and laws of our society. It is where children are *socialized* in very explicit and direct ways. This can make all the difference in the world, concerning whether that society will flourish, or whether it will collapse. Can there be anything more serious than this?

3. *Society as Supporter:*

Given that society derives the major benefit from education, it follows also, our thinkers agree, that it is society which must support education. Far too often, usually for political and economic reasons, governmental support and funding of education is used as a football. Opponents of more support will argue a *laissez-faire* or hands-off policy, belaboring criticisms of teachers and administrators, and even sometimes calling for the privatization of our educational system. The answer, they say, is not more money, but better teachers, better administrators, in short, what can be provided more by the free-market and less by government support. Our thinkers would certainly recommend that financial support coming from the government be guarded against waste and misuse, but they would also point out that since society is the major benefactor, it is only fitting that society (in the form of federal and state governments) foot the bill. And they would emphatically point out that since education is so vitally important, and since teachers are, after all, those who do the educating, it is in the interest of society to make teaching financially attractive enough so that talented persons will continue to be interested in teaching as a profession.

4. *Education as Cooperation:*

Regarding specific styles or forms of education, our thinkers also agree in a number of areas. For example, there is wide support for a more cooperative and less competitive environment in the classroom. It is true, that these great teachers emphasize excellence and achievement, but excellence is best produced, they argue, in an environment which promotes a learning-together model, rather than one which stimulates students to out do each other.

5. *Failures of Traditional Education:*

These thinkers (especially those more contemporary ones, like Dewey and Suzuki) are the first to point out that the traditional approach to education is not working! It is time, therefore, to try another method. In fact, an interesting similarity exists in that our great thinkers were not such great students. They were, often, victimized by the failures of the status quo in education: rote memorization, over-emphasis on testing, etc. Many of them admitted to actually disliking the school environment. What they all realized, however, is that it was not they who failed, but the system which failed them. One can only wonder how many derive a different conclusion. Many students conclude that the failure occurred at a very personal level: they falsely conclude that it is they that have failed and they that will continue to fail throughout their lives! This is a sad commentary on our educational system.

6. *Education as Creative:*

Relevant to this, our thinkers point their collective fingers on just where the failures may lie. Education, they argue, must be much more creative than it has been. Our great thinkers often point out that there is no sin in making the learning environment *fun, natural and useful* to students. Education should be playful and interesting, and an effort should be made to develop techniques which will stimulate the interests of the child.

7. *Education, not Punishment:*

Above all, our thinkers oppose techniques of punishment and a classroom environment which instills fear rather than joy. They point out that it is simply impossible for learning to take place in an atmosphere of anxiety and animosity. Of course, some prohibitions and enforcements thereof are necessary, but even these need not be cloaked only in punishing terms.

8. *Individualized Education:*

Our thinkers do not so much reject a structured classroom as they propose a new kind of structure: one centered more on the individual student, and less on goals-testing for the achievement of averageness. And yes, they are fully aware that this makes more work for the teacher. It is much easier to simply survive in the status quo. Individualized and creative teaching will require creativity and effort from the teacher. And this is just one more reason for making teaching more attractive financially. Our great thinkers realize that we must teach in the real world. And in the real world, all children are not identical, they are not equal, neither in ability nor interest. How can one teach, then, to the abstraction (the generic-average student)? One must attempt to teach to the real child. The child, as an individual, is in need of individual attention.

9. *Education as Involving Both People and Content:*

And this does not mean that our thinkers prefer the student over the subject-matter. Our thinkers are aware that we need not choose between content and people: this is a false dilemma. Of course, content area is important. Our students need to be provided with the tools to carry on their lives and to help society progress into the future. But it is not a matter of rejecting content, it is a matter of recognizing that content cannot be learned by every student in exactly the same way, and at exactly the same pace.

10. *Education as Wholistic:*

Another agreement centers, in fact, on the issue of content. Our thinkers, for example, are very supportive of the importance of arts, music and health education. The life of the mind requires nourishment not only from mathematics and the sciences, it also requires aesthetic food. The arts (literary as well as visual arts) and music are as essentially human and important as the more analytical/rational skills we need to develop. Aesthetic knowledge and enjoyment are not simply luxuries that we should get to when there is time, they are equally important and, for some, the best way to learn. Our thinkers are also aware of the bifurcation (art vs. science) often perpetuated by our educational system. But art and science are related (consider Suzuki here), and the great scientists like Einstein were also accomplished musicians. There is an internal connection, for example, between musical thinking and mathematics. Both involve abstract thinking and creative imagination. Education in health, too, is not seen by our thinkers as some oblique enterprise, but directly necessary and contributing to our overall well being. "A sound mind and a sound body" is the goal of wholistic education.

11. *Education in Character:*

It is because our thinkers are interested in educating the whole person and not just some supposed more important part (the analytical mind, as opposed to the more creative), that they agree, too, that the real purpose of education is the education of character. The character of a person will determine how knowledge is used. Wisdom (the ethical use and understanding of that which I know) is far more important than intelligence. In fact, intelligence becomes potentially dangerous when joined to a bad character. The evil which flowed from an Adolph Hitler, for example, was all the greater because of his innate intelligence. An idiot could not have led such an evil campaign; there was a certain amount of genius displayed in Hitler, but it was a genius without wisdom, a genius that society would be far better left without. It is the business of education, therefore, not just to supply us with smart people, it is the duty of education to supply us with humans who are *humane* members of society. To this purpose, our thinkers would promote education in *virtue* as well as education in *knowledge*. They were also very deeply aware, that at the deepest level, Socrates was right when he taught that *true knowledge is virtue!* The purpose of education is to produce excellence. The Greeks used the word *"arete"* in talking about virtue. *Arete* means excellence, not just in ability but in *action*. And the Greeks understood that excellent action can only come from an excellent character.

12. *Society and Parents as Educators:*

Education has a very important task and mission. Quite possibly, there is no more important task. Our thinkers agree that to carry out this mission, education needs help, not only from the society, but from parents and families in general. Parents and families are teachers as well. Without their support, no educational system can achieve its goals. Education will achieve progress, only if it is recognized that it is a mosaic of relationships: teachers and schools, governments and families, all must work together to produce it--*after all, it is our children and our children's children that are at stake!*

It is remarkable to see that these thinkers, the greatest educational theorists from across the centuries and around the world, share many vital ideas in common. A more detailed study and comparison will no doubt generate more interesting points of agreement and we encourage the reader to use this text only as a good beginning into the very important study into educational theory.

Selected   Bibliography

The following list includes works which are additional to any mentioned in the body of this text and which may provide the reader with additional sources for their own research into theories of education in general, or in particular theorists.

Broudy, Harry S. and Michael J. Parsons, *et al., Philosophy of Education: An Organization of Topics and Selected Sources.* Chicago: University of Illinois Press, 1967. This work offers a very complete bibliography of topics in the philosophy of education.

Brumbaugh, Robert S. and Lawrence, Nathaniel M., *Philosophers on Education: Six Essays on the Foundations of Western Thought.* Boston: Houghton Mifflin, 1963. This text has a good survey of the views of Plato, Aristotle, Rousseau, Kant, Dewey and Whitehead.

Cahn, Stephen M., *The Philosophical Foundations of Education.* New York: Harper and Row, 1970. This text looks at a variety of philosophers from Plato, Aristotle, Locke, Kant, Rousseau, Dewey, Russell, and other contemporary sources.

Dunkel, H.B., *Herbart and Education.* New York: Random House, 1969.

Dunkel, H.B., *Herbart and Herbartianism: An Educational Ghost Story.* Chicago: University of Chicago Press, 1970.

Frankena, William K., *Three Historical Philosophies of Education.* Chicago: Scott Forseman, 1965. This text looks at Aristotle, Kant and Dewey.

Graves, F.P., *Great Educators of the Three Centuries.* New York: The Macmillan Company, 1912.

Harlan, L.R., and Smock, R.W., *The Booker T. Washington Papers (vols. 1-14).* Urbana: University of Illinois Press, 1989.

Hinsdale, B.A., *Horace Mann and the Common School Revival in the United States.* New York: Charles Scribner and Sons, 1913.

Hubbell, G.A., *Horace Mann: Educator, Patriot and Reformer.* Philadelphia: William F. Fell Co., 1910.

Kramer, R., *Maria Montessori.* New York: Putnam and Sons, 1976.

Mann, M.P., *Life of Horace Mann.* Washington: Natural Education Association, 1937.

Massachusetts Department of Education, *Annual Report of the Department of Education Together With the Annual Report of the Society of the Board (12 vols.).* Boston: Dutton and Wentworth, 1837-1848.

McMurray, C.A., *The Elements of General Method.* New York: The MacMillan Co., 1903.

Montessori, Maria, *Childhood Education.* Translated by A.M. Joosten. New York: New American Library, 1955.

Nettleship, R.L., *The Theory of Education in Plato's Republic.* London: Oxford, 1935.

Piaget, Jean, *The Origins of Intelligence in Children.* New York: International University Press, 1952.

Piaget, Jean, *The Construction of Reality in the Child.* New York: Basic Books, 1954.

Painter, F.V.N., *Great Pedagogical Essays.* New York: American Book Co., 1905.

Rogers, Carl, *A Way of Being.* Boston: Houghton Mifflin, 1980.

Scheffler, Israel, *Philosophy and Education.* Boston: Allyn and Bacon, 1966.

Skinner, B.F., *About Behaviorism.* New York: Knopf, 1974.

Skinner, B.F., *The Technology of Teaching.* New York: Appleton-Century Crofts, 1968.

Ulrich, R., *History of Educational Thought.* New York: American Book Co., 1945.

Washington, Booker T., *The Story of the Negro (2 vols.).* New York: Doubleday, Page and Co., 1909.

About the Authors

William Cooney

received the Ph.D. in philosophy from Marquette University. He has also co-authored *Ten Great Thinkers: An Integrative Study in Philosophy and Psychology* (University Press of America) and *Contributions of Gabriel Marcel to Philosophy* (The Edwin Mellen Press), as well as articles on ethics and epistemology in such journals as *Dialogue* and *The Journal of Applied Philosophy.* As associate professor of philosophy at Briar Cliff College (Sioux City, IA), Dr. Cooney is the recipient of the Burlington-Northern Faculty Achievement Award (Teacher of the Year), 1992. His interests include the philosophy of education, the philosophy of mind, ethics, and the philosophy of religion.

Charles Cross

received the Ph.D. in Curriculum and Instruction and a Graduate Gerontology Certificate-Doctoral from The University of Maryland at College Park. He was a recipient of the First Annual Golden ID Student's Association Fellowship for Gerontological Study at the University of Maryland and the George Ellis Moore Award for outstanding scholarship in history at Frostburg State College. Dr. Cross is assistant professor of education at Mount Union College (Alliance, OH). He is an active member of the National Council for the Social Studies (reviewer for *Social Education*), Phi Delta Kappa, Phi Alpha Theta, Association of Teacher Educators, as well as other professional organizations. His interests are in the areas of human relations (multicultural/global education), law-related education, college public school collaboration, educational philosophy, social studies methodology, and issues on aging.

Barry Trunk

is a native of southern California and received his B.A. in Psychology from the University of California, Los Angeles, an M.A. from California State, Long Beach, and the Ph.D., in Developmental Psychology and Psychological Statistics from The Ohio State University. He retired from Briar Cliff College (Sioux City, IA) where he was professor of psychology. He is currently engaged in grief and bereavement counseling and has begun a second career in real-estate sales. He is co-author of *Ten Great Thinkers: An Integrative Study in Philosophy and Psychology* (University Press of America). His many interests include the psychology of music perception and educational theory.